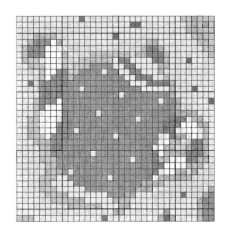

needlepoint

needlepoint

Karen Elder

Photography by Christine Hanscomb

Clarkson Potter/Publishers
New York

Text, design and layout copyright © 1996 Quadrille Publishing Limited
Project photography copyright © 1996 Christine Hanscomb
Detail photography copyright © 1996 Dave King

Published by Clarkson N. Potter/Publishers, 201 East 50th Street, New York, NY 10022. Member of the Crown Publishing Group.

Random House, Inc. New York, Toronto, London, Sydney, Auckland
http://www.randomhouse.com

CLARKSON N. POTTER, POTTER, and colophon are trademarks of Clarkson N. Potter, Inc.

Originally published in Great Britain by Quadrille Publishing Limited in 1996.

Manufactured in Spain.

Library of Congress Cataloging-in-Publication data is available upon request.

ISBN 0-517-88766-5

10 9 8 7 6 5 4 3 2 1

First American Edition

contents

Introduction

To embroider on canvas – or work a piece of needlepoint – is a simple craft. Projects can either be elaborate, requiring skill and imagination to execute, or straightforward, since the most commonly used stitches are effective and easy to learn and there is no particular need to attempt more complicated stitches. The variety of patterns, threads, and canvases alone are enough to keep you occupied for a lifetime.

The hours fly by when you are engrossed in working a piece of needlepoint. Over the centuries needlepoint has been worked as a pastime but has not always been exclusively the province of leisured ladies. The Bradford Table Carpet (early seventeenth century and now housed in the Victoria & Albert Museum, London) was stitched in a workshop and is thought to have been created not as a commissioned work but a product to sell. The amazing set of eighteenth-century chairs at Temple Newsam House in Yorkshire, England, is upholstered in needlepoint, and the skill of its stitching and vibrant coloring suggest that it was made professionally.

In the seventeenth and eighteenth centuries grand houses kept professional embroiderers who also drew patterns for the ladies of the house to execute, because until the early 1800s commercial patterns were not available to buy. The arrival of commercial patterns from Berlin marked the beginning of a long rise in the popularity of needlepoint – or Berlinwork as it was called – in both the United States and England. The patterns were printed on graph paper and hand colored. The development of new dyes at around the same time inspired a fashion for brightly colored floral patterns which is a hallmark of Victorian taste.

Today there are many styles from which to choose. Books have replaced the loose patterns of the last century, and the detailed instructions and lavish illustrations they provide are both informative and inspiring. A wide variety of designs is also available packed in kits containing threads, printed canvas, and needles. But with a charted (as opposed to printed) design, although the difficulties of balancing colors for the designs has already been addressed, the stitcher is still free to add colors or make adjustments to fit a particular need – which is one of the joys of this versatile craft.

Before you start

Choosing the materials for a needlepoint project is simple compared to embarking on other styles of embroidery. The appropriate canvas, thread, needle, and frame are all you need to consider.

The stitches in a needlepoint project usually cover the canvas completely, so the selection of the base fabric is limited to quality and gauge. Most needlepoint is worked in wool threads or cotton floss, and although there are several types available, the choice is not huge. It is wise to use good-quality threads or yarns unless you are experienced, because they are made to withstand the stress of being pulled through the canvas. They are also dyed to a high standard and available in a vast array of colors – a visit to a store that stocks a good range will provide you with inspiration for choosing threads and starting to stitch.

materials & equipment

Needlepoint may require only a minimum of equipment, but it is important that the needle used is the correct size and that the chosen thread covers the selected canvas. A stock of small pieces of different gauge canvases on which to experiment with threads and stitches is an invaluable aid to successful stitching. A selection of embroidery frames in different shapes and sizes (see page 12), although not always essential, can be extremely useful when working a piece of needlepoint.

The workbasket

The essential tools for needlepoint are a selection of needles, scissors, and a tape measure. A pair of small, sharp, pointed scissors is an absolute necessity for cutting threads close to the work. For cutting canvas, you will need a pair of large scissors. Some people like to stitch with a thimble. Apart from these basics, you will need:

• A waterproof marker, for marking the center of the canvas and any outlines or measurements that may be needed. Use a pale-colored marker when working with light thread shades, to prevent the marks from showing through and spoiling the finished design.
• Masking tape, for binding the edges of the canvas to prevent it from fraying and snagging the embroidery thread.

Canvas

Needlepoint canvas is a loosely woven, stiffened fabric usually made from cotton, although linen and synthetic fibers are sometimes used.

Gauge

Hugely varied effects can be achieved by using different "gauges" of canvas: big, chunky cross-stitch on large-holed canvas creates a fabric far removed in texture from the smoothness of tent stitch worked on a fine gauge.

The gauge is the number of holes per 1" (2.5cm), and the standard range runs from 5 to 26 holes per 1" (2.5cm). All the canvases for the projects in the book are listed with their gauge size. Changing the gauge will alter the size of the piece and change its character, so work your needlepoint projects on a gauge close to the canvas size listed.

Widely available canvases:

Mono de luxe	White or ecru	10–18 holes per 1" (2.5cm)
Interlock	White	10–18 holes per 1" (2.5cm)
Large interlock	Cream	7–8 holes per 1" (2.5cm)
Double thread (Penelope)	Ecru	10 holes per 1" (2.5cm)
Double thread (thinner than Penelope)	White	10–14 holes per 1" (2.5cm)
Large double thread (Sudan)	Cream	4–5 holes per 1" (2.5cm)

Types of canvas

There are two main types of canvas: single thread and double thread.

Single-thread canvas

There are two kinds of single-thread canvas:

• Mono, woven with single threads in the warp and weft.

• Interlock, woven with the weft twisted around the warp.

Both types are suitable for most needlepoint projects. However, half cross-stitch (see page 23) is best worked on double-thread canvas, as it holds the stitches more centrally in the holes to give better coverage.

Mono de luxe canvas is the best quality, which is reflected in the price. The threads are polished to provide extra smoothness, and it has the highest tension resistance, making it an ideal choice for chair seats and other projects that will receive heavy wear. It is available in both white and ecru.

Interlock is a strong canvas that is often used for kits, as it is easier to print a needlepoint design on than mono de luxe. Good-quality interlock canvas is suitable for most projects and is mainly available in white.

Double-thread canvas

In double-thread canvas (sometimes called Penelope), the threads are laid two by two, and the embroidery thread is usually passed through the bigger holes. Details, where tiny stitches may be called for, can be worked by separating these double threads to make twice the number of holes, thereby doubling the gauge. However, it is easy to mistakenly push the needle through the wrong hole. Double-thread canvas is available in white and ecru.

Plastic canvas

Plastic needlepoint canvas is also available and is designed for making items with sharp edges that cannot be turned under, such as tissue-box covers and glasses cases. It is available in a variety of useful shapes as well as by the yard (meter) and can be stitched right up to the edge. The outside edges can then be oversewn with no further finishing required. Plastic needlepoint canvas is available in several colors including transparent.

Choosing canvas

The canvas and thread for a project must be selected to suit one another. The thread should run through the holes in the canvas easily, but must also cover it completely. If the canvas shows through the embroidery, then either the thread is not the correct thickness for the canvas gauge or the stitching is too tight.

Although needlepoint canvas is described as an "evenweave" fabric, with the same number of threads in each direction, you may find that there is a slight difference. Therefore, if you are planning to join two pieces of canvas you must make sure that the selvage runs in the same direction for both pieces.

There are a number of canvas manufacturers, and the quality varies. Good-quality canvas should not feel rough (overly stiffened) and should not look hairy in the holes when held up to the light. Rough canvas will strip the embroidery threads and is not pleasant to hold. Although all canvas edges will unravel with use, if it is already unraveling in the store it is best avoided.

Embroidery frames

A frame is an excellent aid for a good finish, because it holds the canvas firmly during stitching. There are many types of frames available, and it is important that the one you choose is strong and does not bend or wobble.

Square or rectangular frames are the best for needlepoint. The canvas, except for very fine-gauge canvases, does not sit well in a hoop (circular) frame.

It is important to decide how you will be sitting at your work – the choice is then narrowed down to a floor-standing frame or one that can be carried around. However, workstands are now available that will hold the frame.

Floor-standing frames

If you always work in the same place, you may consider using a wooden floor-standing embroidery frame. Make sure that you choose a sturdy, good-quality frame that is the right height for your chair. Your hands should not be held so high that they make your shoulders rise.

Slate frames

Professional embroiderers use slate frames. These are not actually made of slate, but they are heavy and strong. The canvas is stitched onto webbing, which is then laced to the side of the frame with a strong thread that allows the canvas to be pulled absolutely taut.

Stretcher frames

Stretcher frames are available from art supply shops (they are really intended for artists' canvases) and some needlework shops. They are sold in pairs of sides which push together at the corners. You can buy a variety of lengths to create different frame sizes. The canvas is held on the frame with tacks.

Roller frames

Roller frames consist of two straight sides joined by two pieces of dowelling, around which the canvas is rolled.

These frames are suitable if you are working in straight lines but not if you are using diagonal tent stitch, because the canvas will be tight where you have worked but loose where you want to stitch. Since the work is rolled, you can only see a part of the canvas at a time – a drawback if creating your own design.

Using a frame

When using a frame, find a position in which to sit where your back is not under strain and that allows you to use both hands for stitching. It is best to sit in an upright chair with both your feet on the floor. Unless you are using a floor-standing frame, sit at a table with the frame weighted down or clamped firmly to the edge.

Your left hand should be on the top of the canvas to push the needle down, with your right hand below to receive the needle and start the next stitch. This may feel strange at first, but once you get into the rhythm it will feel natural.

Working without a frame

Many people stitch happily and successfully without a frame. However, for stitches that stretch over more than two or three threads of canvas, it is advisable to use a frame so that the canvas is kept flat and the right stitch tension is created.

Canvas is stiffened in manufacture to help prevent distortion; good-quality canvas is coated with potato starch, which provides stiffness without coarseness. If you crumple your canvas when working, the stiffening will break up and spoil it; so if you are not using a frame, it is best to roll the canvas and hold the roll between the thumb and fingers of your non-stitching hand. This is comfortable and enables you to complete a whole tent stitch in one step – this is sometimes called "scooping."

Needles

The embroidery needle used for needlepoint is called a "tapestry needle." It has an elongated eye, which is easy to thread, a tapered body, and a blunt, smooth point that is designed to push gently through the needlepoint canvas and past previous stitches, rather than through them. A packet of tapestry needles in assorted sizes is a useful standby in your workbasket.

Choosing the correct needle size will make your work comfortable to manage. Tapestry needles are graded from size 13, for use with the largest-holed rug canvas, up to 26, for use with the finest gauge. The most commonly used are:

Needle size	Canvas gauge
22	16
20	12–14
18	10
16	7–8

Threads and yarns

Wool threads and six-strand cotton floss are the most commonly used threads for working needlepoint. One of the most versatile and widely used needlepoint yarns is Persian-type wool yarn. Silk is also suitable and wonderful to stitch with, but is expensive and not widely available.

There are also numerous "speciality" threads that are fun to use for detailing, or for adding highlight or a bit of sparkle. Beads will add a whole other dimension, or can even be used in place of threads to create "beaded canvaswork."

Wool needlepoint thread is usually packaged in skeins up to 11yd (10m) in length, or in hanks, which are larger and measured by weight. Check the label for length and weight, as these can vary considerably. Cotton floss comes in 8¾yd (8m) skeins.

Tapestry wool

Tapestry wool comes in single-strand form. 4-ply tapestry wool is similar in weight to sport-weight knitting yarn and is easier for inexperienced stitchers to use than stranded wool threads. Most brands of tapestry wool are suited to needlepoint canvas with 10–14 holes per 1" (2.5cm).

Crewel and Persian wools

Stranded threads (both wool and cotton) are extremely versatile, because you can adjust the number of threads to suit the gauge of the needlepoint canvas. Crewel wool is a fine, single-strand thread that can be doubled, tripled, or more to suit different needs.

Persian yarn, so called as it was developed specifically for mending Persian carpets, is slightly thicker and more lustrous than crewel wool, and is made with three strands loosely packed together. The strands are separated easily to be used as required. You will need to experiment to discover the number of strands that best suits the canvas and the type of stitch you are using.

Cotton floss

Cotton embroidery floss is packaged with six strands together. Beginners may find it difficult to get all the strands to run through the canvas evenly – using a frame will help.

Cotton floss is widely available and can be used very successfully on needlepoint canvas (see the Evening Purse on page 88). Cotton floss looks like silk but is inexpensive in comparison to wool embroidery thread. Cotton floss is often used in conjunction with wool thread to work highlights, flower centers, French knots, and other decorative stitches.

Silk threads

Silk threads are not packaged to any standard length or thickness. It is necessary to test silks for coverage and effect before embarking on a project using this beautiful thread.

preparation

A little time spent in preparing your canvas and threads can pay dividends in the long run. Canvas should be cut to the correct size, allowing an extra 2"–3" (5–7cm) margin all around but no more, as it can become unwieldy. Binding the canvas edges with masking tape makes it comfortable to use. Since the canvas should be flat, use an iron to remove any creases and to secure the tape. Finally, sort the threads into color groups and stitch a small piece of each color into the margin of the canvas to aid this process. Seen under electric lights colors are easily mistaken, and this reference can prove invaluable.

Using a chart

Needlepoint patterns for tent stitch, the basic background stitch, can be translated successfully onto graph-paper charts, each square representing a stitch of the work. It is important to note that a stitch goes over a canvas thread intersection, from one hole to the next, not exactly as it looks on the chart – that is, the printed lines on the graph paper do not represent the threads of the canvas. The designs in this book are presented on charts. In color charts the colors may be exaggerated to provide visual differentiation to make them easier to follow. In black-and-white charts a symbol in each square represents the color. Some charts include both symbols and colors.

Positioning the design

When starting to work on an unprinted needlepoint project, the first step is to plan the placement of the design. Find the center of the canvas by folding it in half horizontally and then vertically. The center point is where the creases intersect. Identify the center of the chart. Most charts mark the central axes with an arrowhead in the margin. In order to follow a design without getting lost, it is a good idea to accentuate every tenth line on the graph paper, if it is not already darker. Mark the canvas in the same way, drawing a dotted line very lightly along the warp and weft of the canvas, using a pale-colored waterproof marker. (**Note:** Do not do this if you are using light thread shades, as the marks may show through.) It is then easy to see where you are without continually having to count stitches.

Choosing a kit

When buying a needlepoint kit it is important to look at more than the picture on the packet, because the quality of the materials inside the kit can vary enormously.

A poor quality or badly printed needlepoint canvas is no fun to stitch. Straight lines in the pattern should be reasonably in line with the canvas, but as canvas is a loose-weave fabric there may be some "wandering" of the line. This often worries people, but it should not be difficult to make the necessary adjustments as you stitch.

Blurring of colors, or close shades printed in a way that makes them difficult to distinguish, is a much more serious problem. A good printer will give extra differentiation between the printed colors where wool shades are close; a good designer will also have thought through the printing process, rather than just producing a pretty pattern.

Getting the best from your kit

Figure out which thread shades relate to which printed shades. Most kits have little squares of color printed on the canvas margin; knot a piece of the matching color thread into each square before you start stitching and in artificial light you will not confuse the shades.

Always read the instructions. The designer may have used some surface stitching, or suggested alternative stitches for the background, which cannot be printed.

Transferring designs onto canvas

Printed and painted canvases are widely available, and charts are often available through magazines and books like this one. However, should you wish to trace or paint your own design onto the canvas, it is quite easy. For your first effort it is best to use simple, free-form images and shapes; more complicated patterns can be used when you have gained some experience.

Tracing

Tracing a design onto canvas gives outlines for guidance, but the positioning of colors is left to the stitcher to create freehand. Shading the design on paper to use it as a reference for color placement is helpful.

You will need

Tracing paper
Black felt-tipped pen
Masking tape
Fine-tipped brown or pale gray
    waterproof marking pen

1 When you have chosen your design, mark the center and trace the design onto tracing paper with a black felt-tipped pen, concentrating on the important outlines. Fix the tracing to a flat, clean, white surface using a few short pieces of masking tape.
2 Mark the center of the canvas, then line this up with the center of the design. Fix the canvas on top of the tracing, using small pieces of masking tape.

3 Using a fine-tipped brown or pale gray waterproof marker, lightly trace the design onto the canvas. You can now stitch this marked canvas, putting in the shading "freehand."

Painting

Painting a design onto canvas makes it very easy to stitch. The paints or felt-tipped pens used for this must be waterproof. Tracing the design first can be helpful in insuring that mistakes, which may show through the stitched canvas, are not made.

You will need

Quick-drying, waterproof paint
Fine paintbrush, for details
Larger paintbrush, for more extensive
    areas of color

1 If desired, paint your design on paper before painting the canvas.
2 Fix the design underneath the canvas in the same way as for tracing, and paint it, following the colors on the paper.

from start to finish

Where to begin stitching and how to start and finish an embroidery thread are important, but often unexplained, fundamentals of achieving good needlepoint. Placing the first stitch in the canvas, happy in the knowledge that it is neatly done and will not come loose, is essential for the confidence of the stitcher. With a sure and relaxed hand the stitches will flow across the canvas with an even tension, resulting in a smooth and polishished looking piece of needlepoint.

Threading needles

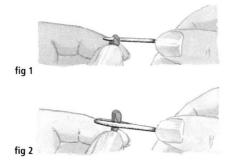

fig 1

fig 2

Threading a needle is something that many people find difficult because of poor eyesight or simply through not knowing an efficient way to do it. Needlepoint needles have large eyes and so are easier to thread than many fine embroidery needles. The easiest way to thread a needle successfully is as follows:

1 Hold the tapestry needle in your right hand (or left if you are left-handed), and with your other hand, loop the thread over the.point of the needle and pull it tight against the needle to make a firm fold in the embroidery thread (fig 1).

2 Holding this loop firmly between your thumb and index finger, turn the needle around, place the eye over the loop and push it down so that the thread passes through it. Do not lick the wool thread: it is unpleasant and achieves little.

Where to start

fig 3

Where you start stitching a piece of needlepoint is important and can differ depending on the pattern and design of the needlepoint.

• For free-form (as opposed to geometric) patterns, start with the main features. This probably means starting in the center and continuing outward until all areas have been stitched.
• For geometric patterns, start at the top right-hand corner (fig 3) and work down the canvas toward the bottom left-hand corner, in a continuous flow.
• If there is a border to the design and you are not using a printed canvas, mark on the canvas where the border should go, using a waterproof marker. Do not jump around when stitching, as you may find that the pattern does not join up successfully if a counting mistake has been made.
• When everything else has been worked, fill in the background. Putting in the background last helps smooth out any unevenness in stitching curves or thin lines. This can be the most exciting phase of the stitching, when everything takes on its proper shape and the colors are offset by the background shade. Start the background at the top (right-hand corner if you are using diagonal tent stitch) and work downward.

Starting a thread

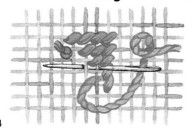

fig 4

The following method of starting is not only safe but beautifully neat and tidy too, as the thread end is worked over underneath the canvas and is covered completely.

1 To start, thread the needle and make a knot right at the end of the thread.
2 Push the needle down through the canvas about ¾" (2cm) away from where you wish to begin, leaving the knot on the front of the canvas.
3 Stitch toward the knot (fig 4), making sure that it is in the "flight path" of your stitching (that is, the direction you will be going), and when you get near the knot, snip it off. The thread underneath will have been neatly worked over.

Threads should be started (and finished) within their own color so that bits of darker fluff do not get caught up with paler shades and spoil them.

Finishing a thread

fig 5

The method used for finishing a thread firmly and neatly varies slightly according to whether you are using wool thread or cotton floss.

• To finish a wool thread, simply run it under several stitches of the same color at the back of the work (fig 5). Wool thread is quite furry and sticks in place when run under just a few stitches.

• Cotton floss and silk thread need to be anchored more firmly. To finish a thread, run it under a few threads of the same color at the back of the work, first in one direction and then the other.

• Snip off all ends as you go to prevent colors from getting tangled, especially where light and dark shades are adjacent. The back of your work will then be neat and tidy.

• Never jump from one area of a color to another, leaving long, loose threads at the back of the canvas – the tension will be wrong and the colors will get tangled with one another. Instead, start and finish a new thread for each area.

Finishing threads on a frame

If you are using a frame – whether fixed or hand held – finishing a thread can be awkward; turning the frame over may be difficult or impossible. A different method can be used:

1 When you have made your last stitch, bring the thread up to the front of the canvas a few stitches away from where you have finished, and somewhere where it will soon be worked over.

2 Trim the thread to about ¾" (2cm), and when it has been worked in underneath, snip it off flush with the canvas.

Achieving a good finish

Perfecting the stitch tension is the most important technique to master in order to achieve an even finish and keep the canvas from becoming distorted. Tight tension can ruin a piece of needlepoint, while a soft, natural tension creates a beautiful and even finish and is relaxing to work. Resist the temptation to give each stitch an extra little tug as you pull the wool thread through – wool thread is slightly elastic and the little tug will stretch it out unnaturally.

The evenness of needlepoint stitches is created by two things: the pulling of the thread as you stitch, and the stitch that shares the hole of the one you have completed. Try to bring your needle up in an empty hole and push it down in a full one. When you push the needle down through a hole where there is a stitch already, the action smooths that stitch. If you start a stitch in a hole that already contains one, you may dislodge that stitch and cause unevenness.

using this book

Chart keys

Color keys are given with the charts for each project. In each key, the first column of shade numbers gives the colors and thread brand used for the original project, and the second column gives the nearest equivalent colors in an alternative brand, although these can be very different.

Canvas gauges

The canvas gauges given in the project instructions indicate the number of holes per inch. See page 10 for a fuller explanation of canvas gauge.

Thread quantities

Every stitcher uses a different amount of thread. The given quantities should be used as a guide only. Some of the pieces are old and the quantities only estimated.

blocking canvas

Canvas worked in tent stitch rarely stays true to its original size and shape, and almost any stitching on canvas benefits from being stretched, or "blocked," back into shape. Tightly stitched canvases that look messy and bumpy are improved enormously by some vigorous blocking treatment, while any slight unevenness in a well-stitched canvas can be quickly eliminated before transforming the stitched canvas into its final use. Follow one of the methods shown here to achieve a smooth needlepoint

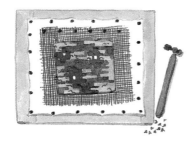

fig 1

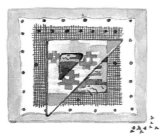

fig 2

You will need
Board at least 6" (15cm) larger in each
 direction than the finished piece
Piece of clean white cotton fabric
Sponge
Heavy-duty thumb tacks, or carpet tacks
 for larger pieces
Hammer
Draftsman's triangle, or other item to
 give a right-angle

1 Pin the white fabric to the board to prevent any stain in the wood from discoloring the work.
2 Dampen the back of the needlepoint using a sponge, but do not saturate it.
3 Lay the needlepoint face down on the board. Tack down the top edge in a straight line (fig 1). Position the tacks in the unstitched canvas margin, about 1" (2.5cm) from the edge of the stitching. If the work is badly out of shape, you may need to put in a tack every inch (2.5cm) or even closer. Put the first tack in the center of the top edge and work outward in both directions.
4 Place tacks in the centers of the other three unstitched canvas margins, starting at the bottom. Use the draftsman's triangle to check that the corners are all at right angles (fig 2). You may have to pull the canvas hard.
5 Once the work has been secured, leave for at least a week until thoroughly dry.

Blocking small pieces

There is an alternative, unconventional, but effective and less physically demanding method for blocking pieces of work no larger than 20" (50cm) square. (**Note**: Do not use this method on valuable or delicate pieces.)

You will need
Powdered wallpaper paste and brush
Artist's stretcher frame (see page 12)
 large enough for the untrimmed
 canvas
Heavy-duty thumb tacks, or carpet tacks
 for larger pieces
Electric kettle, or other piece of
 equipment to produce steam
Rubber gloves

1 Mix up a small amount of wallpaper paste to make a thick, non-watery solution and set aside.
2 Using two chairs, trestles, or sturdy boxes, create a stand on which the frame can be placed flat over the steamer, so that the steam rises to dampen the canvas. The steam should come from about 8" (20cm) below the canvas.

3 Tack the canvas to the stretcher. The tacks should be about 1" (2.5cm) away from the edge of the stitched needlepoint canvas; closer if possible.
4 Place the stretcher over the kettle or steamer, with the wrong side face down (fig 3). This should not be dangerous, but for safety's sake you should wear rubber gloves and insure that your arms are covered, as the steam can scald. After about a minute in the steam the canvas should be pliable, and you will be able to pull the stretcher frame into shape until the canvas is perfectly square. Leave in the steam for another minute and then switch off the kettle or steamer.
5 Brush the wallpaper paste onto the wrong side of the stitched area.
6 Leave flat for about a week to dry out thoroughly. (**Note**: Do not press!)

fig 3

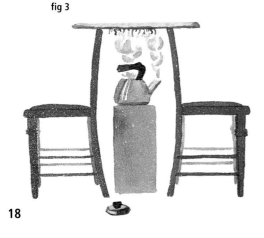

caring & storing

Needlepoint should last for many lifetimes if good-quality materials are used and the correct stitches are selected for the chosen project. The biggest enemies are dust and sunlight. Although modern wool threads are colorfast to a high degree, over the life of a piece some fading must be expected. Leaving needlepoint in a sunny spot will certainly spoil the colors, so bear this in mind when placing pieces around the house or displaying framed needlepoint pictures.

Cleaning

The best way to care for your needlepoint is to spray it well with a fabric protector as soon as it is made up and then use a vacuum cleaner on it regularly. Dampening it or using solvents may remove the natural oils in the wool that are its best protection.

Only clean your needlepoint when it is really necessary – which is less often than you may think – and then send it to a good dry cleaner. Never wash your work: the canvas may shrink and the wool become matted, and if it is a printed or painted canvas there is a chance that the color may run. In addition, washing removes the canvas dressing, which may be keeping the work in shape.

Storing

The best way to store needlepoint is to shake or vacuum it well to remove any dust and then lie it flat (or rolled if it is a large or long piece) in a drawer, wrapped in acid-free tissue paper. Do not use plastic bags, because the static attracts dust and the textiles will not be able to breathe. Place a mothball in the drawer where it will not touch any of the fabric. Finally, lay a piece of white cotton fabric over the top.

Tent stitch

The most frequently used stitch in needlepoint is "tent" stitch, in which the canvas is covered by stitches that cross one thread of canvas diagonally. This is the most versatile of all the needlepoint stitches, and there is no need to learn additional stitches if you are happy with it, for there are worlds of shading, pattern, and color manipulation to be explored using just this one stitch. Figurative, abstract, and geometric patterns can all be formed successfully with tent stitch, and with experience its limitations become challenges of ingenuity and skill. Making straight lines appear to be curves, deceiving the eye with apparent textural effects, and using imaginative shading techniques are just some of the fun possible with tent stitch.

working tent stitch

Tent stitch is formed by bringing the thread up through a hole in the canvas and down through the hole diagonally opposite. This stitch is also called *petit point*, but this is not, as the name suggests, a tiny stitch – nor is *gros point* a big stitch. *Petit point* is tent stitch and *gros point* is cross stitch, on canvas of any size.

People are sometimes timid about stitching details when using any but the finest gauge canvases. However, there is no need to use a 22 gauge to make a face or curve a petal, for it is only an impression that is being created by needlepoint. A pattern stitched on a very fine gauge canvas will usually adapt perfectly to a large gauge, and vice versa.

There are three commonly used ways of forming tent stitch: diagonal tent stitch, continental tent stitch, and half cross-stitch.

Left-handed stitchers

Most left-handed people stitch using their right hand, working in the same way as right-handers do. However, those who do stitch using their left hand may find it easier to work tent stitch with the stitches lying from top left to bottom right, rather that the more usual top right to bottom left. If working diagonal tent stitch, start at the top left-hand corner of the pattern. If using continental tent stitch or half cross-stitch, start wherever it feels most comfortable. Remember that it is not a question of "right" and "wrong" ways of stitching, as long as the required effect is achieved and the stitcher is comfortable with the chosen techniques.

Diagonal tent stitch

Sometimes called "basketweave" because of the pattern it creates on the back of the work, diagonal tent stitch consists of rows of stitching that run diagonally up and down the canvas on the "cross" of the fabric, working toward the top of the design on the up row and toward the right-hand edge on the down row. Each stitch fills a gap between the stitches of the previous row.

1 Starting at the top right-hand corner of the area to be covered, bring the needle up through the canvas at the bottom of the stitch and down in the hole above and diagonally to the right (fig 1).
2 Make the next stitch parallel to the first and stitch the row going diagonally up or down the canvas as required. The small gaps between the stitches will be filled when the next row is worked.
3 Work the next row below the first (fig 2), bringing the the needle up in the empty canvas and down between the stitches of the row above (fig 3).

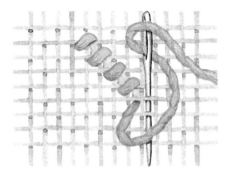

fig 1

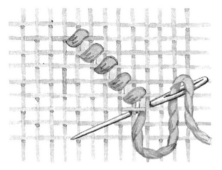

fig 2

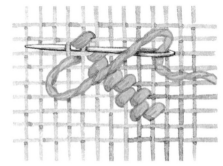

fig 3

Continental tent stitch

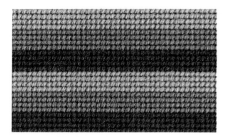

This variation consists of rows of stitching that travel in straight lines backwards and forward across the canvas, forming long diagonal stitches at the back.

1 Working the first row from right to left, bring the needle up through the canvas at the bottom of the stitch and down in the hole above and diagonally to the right (fig 4).

2 Making a long stitch at the back of the work, bring the needle up again to the left of the first stitch, and continue.

3 Work the second row from left to right (fig 5), this time bringing the needle up through the canvas at the top of the stitch and down in the hole below and diagonally to the left (fig 6), making long diagonal stitches at the back.

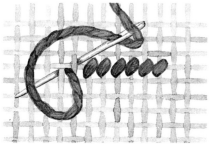

fig 4

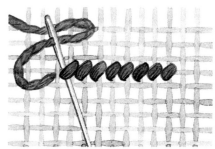

fig 5

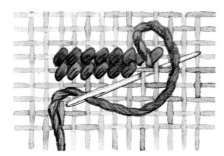

fig 6

Half cross-stitch

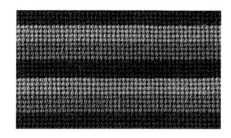

Technically, this method is not a tent stitch, but it looks the same on the front of the work. It is formed by stitching in straight lines across the canvas, but creating a short, vertical stitch at the back.

1 Working the first row from left to right, bring the needle up through the canvas at the bottom of the stitch and down through the hole diagonally above and to the right (fig 7).

2 Making a small straight stitch at the back of the work, repeat step 1.

3 Work the second row of half cross-stitch from right to left (fig 8), bringing the needle up through the needlepoint canvas at the top of the stitch and down in the hole below and diagonally to the left (fig 9), making small straight stitches at the back of the work.

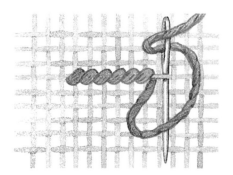

fig 7

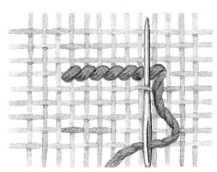

fig 8

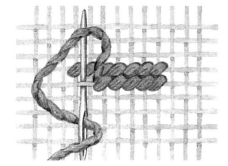

fig 9

boat pictures

These three little boat pictures, each framed using old pieces of wood with peeling paint, have an immediate, rustic appeal. They make a refreshing change from mass-produced decorative arts, as no two frames can ever be the same.

The designer is left-handed and he has therefore slanted the stitches from top left to bottom right, as opposed to the more usual top right to bottom left: either way works well. If you want to follow exactly what the designer has done, turn the chart on its side so that the top left becomes top right.

Three fishing boats

About the picture

Approximate finished design size: 6¾" x 3" (17cm x 7cm). The picture shown was worked in Anchor tapestry wool.

You will need

14-gauge interlock or mono de luxe canvas, 11" x 7" (27 x 18cm)
Size 20 tapestry needle
Tapestry wool in the Anchor or Rowan colors listed in the key below

To work all the needlepoint designs

The designs are all worked in tent stitch. The continental tent-stitch method is recommended, as the lined effect that it gives adds an appropriate texture to the seascapes. Stitch the boats first and then the backgrounds.

When stitching the steamer, use all six strands of floss throughout. Frame the completed pictures as desired.

Note: The charts for the steamer and yacht pictures are on pages 98 and 99.

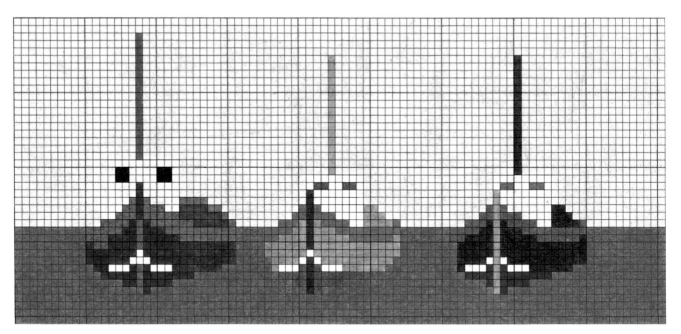

Tapestry wool	Anchor	Rowan	skeins
■ black	9800	A62	1
▨ gray	9798	A625	1
▨ soft gray	9764	Z61	1
■ dark greenish blue	8840	M54	1
■ cherry red	8220	G46	1

Tapestry wool	Anchor	Rowan	skeins
▨ maroon	8512	H659	1
■ brown	9410	X146	1
■ soft brown	9392	J427	1
▨ ginger	8062	D620	1
▨ orange	8162	C618	1

Tapestry wool	Anchor	Rowan	skeins
☐ fawn	9362	A2	1
☐ white	8006	A110	1
☐ sky blue	8736	N422	1
■ sea blue	8738	N88	1
▨ green	8880	P100	1

Yacht

About the picture

Approximate finished size of the blocked needlepoint picture: 3" x 3½" (7 x 9cm).

The picture shown was worked in Anchor tapestry wool.

You will need

14-gauge interlock or mono de luxe canvas, 7" x 7½" (17 x 19cm)

Size 20 tapestry needle

Tapestry wool in the colors listed in the key (see pages 98 and 99)

Steamer

About the picture

Approximate finished design size: 3¼" x 1½" (8 x 4cm).

The picture shown was worked in DMC cotton floss except for the sea, which uses Anchor.

You will need

17-gauge interlock canvas, 7¼" x 5½" (18 x 14cm)

Size 26 tapestry needle

Cotton floss in the colors listed in the key (see pages 98 and 99)

circus pillow

The bold colors and inventive subject make this a lovely design for a playroom or child's bedroom. The three figures look as if they come from flip cards, depicting heads, torsos, and legs that can be mixed and matched to create hundreds of different and unlikely characters. This humorous design is set in a festive border of stars, circles, hearts, and zigzags that defy boredom in the stitching. There is neither shading nor any complicated coloring, making this a good design for a beginner to tackle.

About the pillow
Approximate finished size: 14" (34cm) square. The pillow shown was worked in Anchor tapestry wool.

You will need
For the needlepoint:
10-gauge double-thread (Penelope) canvas, 20" (50cm) square
Size 18 or 20 tapestry needle
Tapestry wool in the Anchor or DMC colors listed in the key on page 28
For the pillow:
1¼yd (1m) medium-weight cotton upholstery fabric, 48" (122cm) wide
12" (30cm) zipper
Sewing thread to match fabric
60" (1.5m) piping filler cord
16" (40cm) square pillow form

To work the needlepoint
The design is worked in tent stitch. Use your preferred method.

With this busy design there is no reason for any particular order of stitching, but the general rule is to work from the center, so stitch the figures first and then the frames in which they are

fig 1

set. Stitch the border when the whole central section is complete.

To finish the pillow
1 Block the completed canvas, and trim the unstitched canvas margin to approximately ¾" (2cm) all around.
2 Cut the backing fabric into 2 pieces, each 16" x 9" (40 x 22cm).
3 Place the 2 pieces of fabric right sides together, and lay the zipper along the cut line in a central position. Mark where the zipper starts and finishes, and machine stitch to the mark at each end, taking a ¾" (2cm) seam allowance.
4 Lay the fabric flat on an ironing board, face down. Press open the 2 short seams. Press the seam allowances to the wrong side along the zipper opening. Baste and then machine stitch the zipper in place. Partially open the zipper.
5 Cut out a 2½" (6cm) wide strip of fabric on the bias (diagonally across the grain), approximately 3" (7cm) longer than the outer edge of the pillow. With wrong sides together, fold the strip in half lengthwise over the piping filler cord, and baste to hold it in place (fig 1).

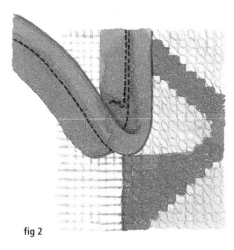

fig 2

6 Pin the piping to the right side of the needlepoint so that it covers the first three rows of stitching; this allows the seam to run right along the edge of the stitching (fig 2). Machine stitch an inch (a few centimeters) to check that the placement is correct, and adjust if necessary.

7 Machine stitch the piping in place all around the needlepoint, clipping the piping seam allowance at each corner so that it does not pull. Hand sew the ends together to fit.

8 With right sides together, pin and baste the backing fabric to the needlepoint. The piping will be caught in between and will cause the fabric to be quite tight across the back. Using a zipper foot, machine stitch around the edge, keeping close to the piping.

9 Machine stitch again just around the corners. Trim the corners of the seam allowances diagonally.

10 Turn the cover right side out. Ease out the corners, using a knitting needle to push them out if necessary. Insert the pillow form, and close the zipper.

Tapestry wool	Anchor	DMC	skeins
cream	8004	Ecru	3
light yellow	8112	7471	3
bright yellow	8116	7433	1
red	8216	7666	3
bright orange	8166	7740	2
light orange	9444	7917	1
pale orange	9522	7171	3
pink	8394	7132	1
mauve	8524	7253	2
turquoise	8802	7828	2
peacock blue	8690	7317	1
charcoal	9768	7624	2
bright green	9154	7341	2

album cover

An album of memories is very personal, but some have boring or even ugly covers that belie the sentiment and nostalgia of the contents. Giving an album an individual and hand-made cover makes it truly your own. This one is covered in a natural, coarse-weave linen fabric with a strip of antique needlepoint applied for decoration.

About the cover

Approximate finished motif size: 4¼" x 1½" (10.5 x 4cm)
The length of the stitched needlepoint strip should be equal to the height of the album. The instructions are for an album 11" x 12" (28 x 30cm). The album border shown was worked in Appletons tapestry wool. Adjust the quantities of the materials listed to suit the album of your choice.

You will need

For the needlepoint:
10-gauge double-thread (Penelope) canvas, 6" x 16" (15 x 40cm)
Size 18 or 20 tapestry needle
Tapestry wool in the Appletons or DMC colors listed in the key on the left
For the cover:
Photograph album
12" x 24" (30 x 60cm) lightweight polyester batting
15" x 38" (38 x 96.5cm) natural linen fabric
1¼yd (1m) piping filler cord
3" x 30" (7 x 75cm) bias strip of red cotton fabric
Sewing thread to match fabrics
Fabric adhesive
Tailor's chalk

To work the needlepoint

The design is worked in tent stitch, and the diagonal method is recommended. Work the strawberries and leaves first, and then the background.

To finish the cover

1 Block the completed canvas, and trim the unstitched canvas margin to approximately ¾" (2cm) all around.
2 Make two 14¼" (36cm) lengths of piping, following step 5 of the instructions for the Circus Pillow on page 26.
3 Pin and baste the piping along the edges of the canvas following steps 6 and 7 of the instructions for the Circus Pillow on page 28. Machine stitch the piping in place.
4 Turn under and machine stitch a ½" (1.5cm) hem all around the linen fabric. With the right side out, wrap the fabric around the closed album, leaving 2 flaps of equal length protruding over the edges. Using tailor's chalk, mark on the fabric where the album ends.
5 Baste the needlepoint strip to the fabric 2" (5cm) in from the marked edge. Machine stitch, positioning the needle between the piping and the needlepoint edge. Alternatively, slipstitch by hand underneath the piping.
6 Fold back the 2 fabric flaps along the marked line (the needlepoint will be covered). Pin, baste, and machine stitch each flap along top and bottom with a ¾" (2cm) seam allowance, to form 2 pockets. Turn these right side out, and press to neaten seams and edges.
7 Glue the batting to the album cover, using fabric adhesive. Allow to dry.
8 Slip the fabric cover over the album. Fold the fabric margin to the inside of the album spine and glue to hold the cover firmly in place.

Tapestry wool	Appletons	DMC	skeins
dark green	548	7379	1
olive green	347	7393	1
mid green	345	7376	1
light green	343	7362	1
pale green	341	7424	1
yellow	693	7472	1
wine red	505	7199	1
scarlet	504	7127	1
red	503	7108	1
light red	223	7851	1
ecru	691	7491	3

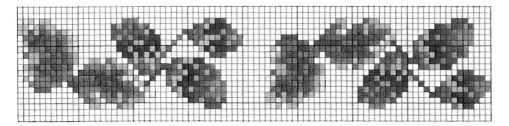

kelim pillow

Inspiration for creating successful needlepoint patterns is never far away, and traditional furnishings provide an endless source of suitable patterns. Indian rugs are especially rich in colors and geometric shapes that work particularly well in needlepoint, as they were designed for wool and therefore lose little in the translation from weaving to embroidery.

About the pillow

Approximate finished size: 22¾" x 23" (57 x 58cm). The pillow shown was worked in Appletons tapestry wool.

You will need

For the needlepoint:
7- or 8-gauge interlock canvas 28" (70cm) square
Size 16 tapestry needle
Tapestry wool in the Appletons or Anchor colors listed in the key on page 34
For the pillow:
24" x 26" (60 x 65cm) medium-weight upholstery fabric
Matching sewing thread
20" (50cm) zipper
3yd (2.5m) cord trim (optional)
Buttonhole thread (optional)
26" (65cm) square pillow form

To work the needlepoint

The design is worked in tent stitch. Use 2 strands of yarn in the needle throughout. The pattern is built up in bands. Stitch one band at a time, working from the top right-hand corner across the canvas. Finish one band before starting the next, otherwise the pattern may not fit correctly. Rigorous counting of the stitches on the chart is not necessary.

To finish the pillow

1 Block the completed canvas, and trim the unstitched margin ¾" (2cm).
2 Cut out 2 pieces of backing fabric, 24" x 20" (60 x 50 cm) and 24" x 6" (60 x 15cm).

3 Insert the zipper in the backing fabric, following steps 3 and 4 of the instructions for the Circus Pillow on page 26.
4 With right sides together and the needlepoint uppermost, pin, baste, and machine stitch the backing fabric to the needlepoint. The machine stitches should run down the middle of the last line of stitching. After sewing along one side, check that you have not encroached on the stitching and also that there is no unstitched canvas showing, and adjust as necessary.
5 Complete by following steps 9 and 10 of the instructions for the Circus Pillow on page 28.

To attach the trim (optional)

1 Snip the bottom seam of the pillow to make an opening approximately 2½" (6cm) long.
2 Using buttonhole thread or sewing thread doubled, slipstitch the cord to the pillow, starting at the opening created in step 1 and stitching along the seam. The stitches should be made quite close together but should not be pulled tight, as this may cause the canvas to pucker. Leave 2½" (6cm) of cord free for making a neat join.
3 When the stitching is complete, tuck the 2 ends through the opening.
4 Trim off the cord ends inside to approximately 2" (5cm), and gently unwind the cord ends inside.
5 On the outside of the pillow, overlap the cord ends where they meet to make a neat join, and stitch firmly in place.

Tapestry wool		Appletons	Anchor	skeins
	biscuit	764	9492	9
	custard	851	9522	12
	deep yellow	474	8136	8
	honeysuckle	696	8102	7
	gray-green	354	9174	2
	deep green	294	9078	2
	flamingo	626	8162	3
	coral	866	8240	20
	scarlet	505	8220	10
	royal blue	821	8688	11
	deep royal blue	823	8690	4
	china blue	748	8634	18
	marine blue	328	8840	11

35

tea cozy

This jolly tea cozy is a good project for a beginner since it is not too large and the motifs are simple, making it quick to complete. It is also a good piece for freeing the mind from the rigors of counted patterns, where every stitch must be placed correctly, and the freedom of the wavy border should discourage you from feeling that you have made mistakes if the stitching is not reproduced exactly as the chart indicates. The randomly placed dots in the background are a clever device for breaking up areas of solid color.

About the cozy

Approximate finished design size: 9½" x 12½" (24 x 31cm). The tea cozy was worked in Anchor tapestry wool. Light blue gingham was used to line the tea cozy, and it complements the design.

You will need

For the needlepoint:
10-gauge double-thread (Penelope) canvas, 16" x 18" (40 x 45cm)
Size 18 or 20 tapestry needle
Tapestry wool in the Anchor or DMC colors listed in the key on page 38
For the cozy:
20" (50cm) medium-weight cotton backing fabric, 36" (90cm) wide
Two 15" x 12" (38 x 30cm) pieces lightweight cotton, for lining
Sewing thread to match fabrics
28" (70cm) piping filler cord (optional)
Two 15" x 12" (38 x 30cm) pieces of medium-weight batting

To work the needlepoint

The design is worked in tent stitch, and the diagonal method is recommended.

Stitch the motifs and the border first, then work the dark blue dots in the background. These require some long stitches to be carried over the back, but the threads will be covered when the background is filled in. However, avoid carrying the loose thread over more than 1" (2.5cm). Fill in the background last.

To finish the cozy

1 Block the completed canvas thoroughly (it is very important that it is straight), and trim the unstitched canvas margin to about ¾" (2cm) all around.

2 Make the piping from the backing fabric, following step 5 for the Circus Pillow on page 26.

3 With the right side of the needlepoint uppermost, pin and baste the piping cord around the curve of the cozy. The basting stitches should be positioned exactly where the machine stitching will eventually run. Make sure that no unstitched canvas is showing.

4 Cut a strip of backing fabric 5½" x 2½" (14 x 6cm). Press the long raw edges to the center, then press in half lengthwise. Topsitch 3 rows of evenly spaced stitches along the folded strip. Fold in half to form a loop, and pin to the center top of the cozy over the piping.

5 Place the needlepoint on the cotton backing fabric, and mark around the edge using tailor's chalk, with a ¾" (2cm) seam allowance all around. Use this shaped piece of fabric to cut out 2 more pieces of lightweight fabric and batting for the lining.

6 Place the needlepoint and backing fabric right sides together; the piping and loop will be sandwiched in between. Using a zipper foot, machine stitch right up against the edge of the piping. Remove any basting stitches that may be showing.

7 Baste a piece of batting to one side of each lining piece. Stitch the 2 pieces of lining fabric together along the curve, leaving a small opening for turning. Then machine stitch the bottom edges to the bottom edges of the cozy. Turn cozy right side out. Then slipstitch the opening closed.

8 Push the lining up inside the cozy; hold with a few stitches at the top of the cozy.

Tapestry wool	Anchor	DMC	skeins
bright pink	8454	7603	1
red	8440	7849	1
orange	8306	7951	2
pale gold	8038	7503	2
bright yellow	8114	7431	1
green	9112	7382	1
pale green	9092	7400	1
turquoise	8802	7828	1
powder blue	8684	7800	5
sky blue	8644	7798	1
dusky blue	8628	7283	1
lilac	8586	7241	1
pale gray	9782	7300	1
cream	8032	Ecru	1

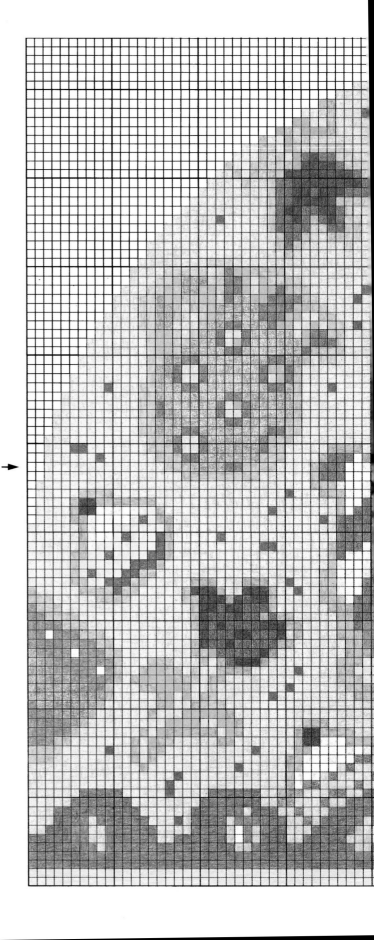

bobble-edged pillow

Oversized blooms, reminiscent of Dutch flower paintings, look wonderful in needlepoint and are especially suitable for upholstery, as the pattern can be used as a length of fabric rather than as a design. This bobble-edged pillow has been made using this technique, and the pattern makes a welcome change from designs contained within borders.

The shading of the flowers and foliage is especially interesting. A very large number of colors has been used and the tones are often unexpected. For example, the big pink flower uses reds, grays, greens, yellow, and white – with some pink. The overall impression, however, is not of a multicolored flower, but of a pink one with the underside of the petals darker than the top. The darker shades are used for the leaves, and the red is also used to shade the yellow flowers.

About the pillow
Approximate finished design size 14" (34cm) square. The pillow shown was worked in Appletons tapestry wool. Rust red, ribbed upholstery cotton was used to make the pillow shown.

You will need
For the needlepoint:
10-gauge double-thread (Penelope) canvas, 20" (50cm) square
Size 18 or 20 tapestry needle
Tapestry wool in the Appletons or Anchor colors listed in the key on page 42
For the pillow:
20" (50cm) square of medium-weight upholstery fabric
12" (30cm) zipper
Sewing thread to match fabric
60" (1.5m) bobble trim
16" (40cm) square pillow form

To work the needlepoint
The design is worked in tent stitch. Use your preferred method.

Work the largest flowers first, then the leaves and small flowers, and finally the background.

To finish the pillow
1 Block the completed canvas, and trim the unstitched canvas margin to approximately ¾" (2cm).
2 Cut the backing fabric into 2 pieces and insert the zipper, following steps 3–4 for the Circus Pillow on page 26.
3 With right sides together and the canvas uppermost, baste and then machine stitch the backing fabric to the needlepoint. The machine stitches should run down the middle of the last line of stitching *unless* you are using a bobble trim (see below). After stitching along one side, check that you have not encroached on the stitching and also that there is no unstitched canvas showing, and adjust if necessary.
4 Complete by following steps 9 and 10 of the instructions for the Circus Pillow on page 28.

To attach the trim
1 Make the pillow cover as above, but instead of stitching down the middle of the last line of stitching, leave an unstitched canvas margin to match the width of the trim.
2 When the pillow is complete, stitch on the trim over the unstitched canvas. To accommodate the corner, make a pleat or tuck in the trim. Fold under the cut ends before stitching down. Pin on the bobble trim before you start stitching and adjust to insure that the bobbles are evenly placed at each corner.

Tapestry wool		Appletons	Anchor	skeins					
■	coral	866	8240	2	■	mid terracotta	223	8348	2
■	pale flame	204	8324	1	□	pale mauve	883	8582	1
■	terracotta	124	9620	2	□	ivory	871	8032	1
■	beige	121	9596	2	■	olive green	342	9054	1
■	dark paprika	726	9564	1	■	dark green	358	9182	1
■	paprika	725	9562	2	■	green	355	9176	2
■	pale paprika	721	9512	1	■	gray-green	351	9254	1
■	biscuit	765	9448	2	■	pale fawn	951	9364	1
■	fawn	912	9388	1	■	jacobean green	298	9026	1
■	honeysuckle	695	8060	1	■	mid jacobean green	296	9082	1
■	golden brown	903	9426	2	■	beige green	292	9066	3
■	gray	962	9788	1	■	dark olive green	245	9220	2
■	rose pink	141	9614	2	■	blue	159	8906	3
□	pale chocolate	181	9632	1	■	deep yellow	475	8102	1
■	autumn yellow	476	9526	1					

house, heart, & hand pillows

Hands and hearts appear as symbolic motifs in many cultures. They are associated particularly with the Shaker movement, one of their sayings being "Hands to work and hearts to God." The little schoolhouse motif is also associated with the Shakers and nineteenth-century American country-style folk art.

These designs must be worked with a fine wool thread, as the subtle, faded effect is created by threading two different-colored wools into the needle at the same time.

About the pillows

Approximate finished size: 9" (23cm) square. The pillow shown was worked in Paternayan Persian yarn.

Note: See pages 100 and 101 for the outline design for the heart and hand pillows. These can be worked using the same stranded yarn colors as for the house pillow.

You will need for each pillow

For the needlepoint:
10-gauge double-thread (Penelope) canvas, 12" (30cm) square
Size 18 or 20 tapestry needle
Stranded yarn in the Paternayan Persian yarn or Appletons crewel wool colors listed in the key on page 47
For the pillow:
Piece of denim approximately 1¼" (3cm) larger than the design all around
Sewing thread to match fabric
Loose polyester stuffing

Stranded yarn	Paternayan	Appletons	skeins
cranberry	940	948	1
spice	850	866	1
cranberry	940	948	1
dark rust	870	127	1
terracotta	482	721	1
spice	850	866	1
terracotta	482	721	1
pale rust	873	206	1
rusty rose	934	753	1
flesh pink	494	704	1
old gold	754	693	1
honey gold	735	692	1
honey gold	735	692	1
white	263	991	1
old blue	510	926	1
old blue	510	926	1
federal blue	503	322	1
glacier blue	563	741	3
blue	561	745	3

To work all the needlepoint designs

The needlepoint design is worked in tent stitch, and the diagonal method is recommended. Start with the central motifs, and then stitch the background. Use 2 strands of Paternayan Persian yarn (or 3–4 strands of Appletons crewel wool) throughout. Combine the colors as indicated in the key.

To finish the pillows

1 Block the completed canvas, and trim the unstitched canvas margin to approximately ¾" (2cm) all around.
2 With right sides together and the needlepoint uppermost, pin, baste, and machine stitch the denim and needlepoint together. The needle should run along the last line of stitching – check after the first 6" (15cm) to insure that you have placed it correctly. The edge of the stitching should meet the denim exactly: too close, and you will not produce a crisp seam; too far away, and the canvas will show. Start and finish about 2" (5cm) in from the bottom corners, thus leaving an opening along the bottom edge.
3 Machine stitch 2 further rows of stitching around the corners, and then trim the fabric and canvas diagonally across the corners.
4 Turn the pillow right side out, and ease out the corners, using a knitting needle to push them out gently.
5 Fill the pillow with stuffing, pushing it well into the corners, and slipstitch the opening closed by hand.

47

Cross-stitch

Cross-stitch is often used as an alternative to tent stitch and is enjoying something of a revival, probably engendered by the renewed popularity of the flower and fruit patterns that are associated with the Berlin woolwork of the turn of the century, which usually employed this stitch. This is cross-stitch at its simplest, sewn over one thread of canvas in each direction, which makes it double the thickness of the ordinary tent stitch and therefore well suited to soft-furnishing decorative accents made from canvas embroidery. However, cross-stitch is not limited to this one form and can be worked in a number of different decorative versions, from double cross-stitch to oblong cross-stitch, each useful for producing a specific finished effect.

working cross-stitch

Cross-stitch has two important attributes: its hardwearing finish, and the fact that it distorts the canvas very little, which can be especially useful if you are stitching a rug made up of squares that are to be sewn together. In addition, if you stitch with even tension there may be no distortion at all, and the piece will not need to be worked on a frame. The drawbacks to cross-stitch are that it uses more yarn or embroidery thread and also takes longer to work than tent stitch.

Cross-stitch variations are numerous and can make interesting backgrounds for geometric patterns. They are also useful where added texture is required. With some forms of cross-stitch the canvas shows through, intentionally, which creates an almost lacy effect.

Working the stitches

Cross-stitch is worked in straight lines backward and forward across the canvas. Be sure to keep the top stitch of each cross facing in the same direction, otherwise the finished piece will look messy.

In geometric and multi-stitch designs, the pattern may dictate that the top stitches face in different directions, but these changes are carefully planned and should be followed closely to insure that the patterning is not confused by top stitches worked the wrong way around, as this results in a sloppy finish.

Stitches may be carried over more than one canvas thread (fig 5, right), as in the border of the Sampler on page 92, where they are worked over two canvas threads in each direction.

Canvas gauge

Canvas gauge in relation to the thread or yarn selected is an important consideration when using cross-stitch, as four strands of thread will have to fit into each hole. If the holes are too small, the stitches will be too tight, creating a bumpy finish; too large, and the coverage will be poor, leaving holes between the stitches. For this reason too, cross-stitch is best worked on a mono rather than double-thread canvas.

As a general rule, 10-gauge canvas works well with single-thread tapestry wool; the yarn can be doubled for working on a 7/8-gauge canvas. If you are using finer stranded threads, stitch some small test pieces to find the number of strands that will best cover your chosen canvas.

Cross-stitch

The usual method of working the crosses in needlepoint is to complete each cross-stitch before starting the next one. All the top stitches should be lying in the same direction.

1 Make a tent stitch, bringing the needle up through the canvas and down diagonally above, to the left (fig 1).

2 Complete the cross by making a stitch that crosses the first one and lies in the opposite direction (fig 2).

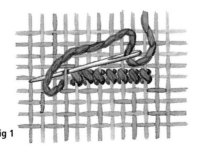

fig 1

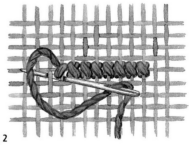

fig 2

Oblong cross-stitch

This stitch is made in the same way as cross-stitch (left) but the stitch is elongated, crossing more threads of canvas in one direction than the other (figs 3 and 4).

Oblong cross-stitch may be worked in rows starting from the left or the right. Double oblong is oblong cross-stitch with another stitch made across the center. The end result looks like lines of little haystacks.

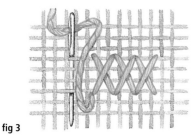

fig 3

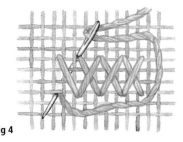

fig 4

Long-armed cross-stitch

In this stitch, the stitches are connected by the long arm, which stretches across into the adjacent stitch to create an interesting and complex texture (figs 5 and 6).

Long-armed cross-stitch must be worked in horizontal rows from left to right, starting each row anew. It should be used as a stitch on its own – or in a striped design – as it will not fit around or against other needlepoint stitches.

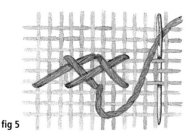

fig 5

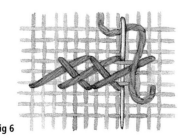

fig 6

Double cross-stitch

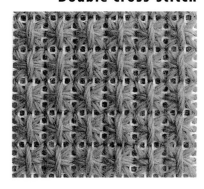

Also known as the Smyrna cross-stitch, double cross-stitch consists of a basic cross-stitch as described left, with another cross made over the top in horizontal and vertical directions (figs 7 and 8).

In two colors, it produces a striking effect. The illustration shows it worked on a gauge whereby the canvas shows through, which can be decorative. Thicker thread or a smaller gauge will give more dense coverage.

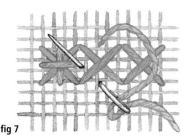

fig 7

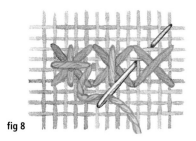

fig 8

51

art deco bag

This little bag displays art deco style at its most charming and was copied from an original 1930s design. The colors are bright but soft and are used straight, with no subtle shading or depth of tone; nevertheless, the finished effect is very sophisticated. The lining has been attached to the metal clasp with a clever little ruffle to cover what would otherwise be an ugly joint, creating a pretty and unusual finishing touch.

It is essential that the stitched canvas pieces are not distorted. If mishapen in any way, the two sides would pull against one another in different directions – even a small amount of distortion will spoil the finish. For this reason, cross-stitch is the best choice.

About the bag

Approximate finished size:
6" x 6¾" (15 x 17cm). The bag shown was worked in Paternayan Persian yarn.

You will need

For the needlepoint:
13-gauge interlock or mono de luxe
 canvas, 14½" x 20" (35 x 50cm)
Size 20 tapestry needle
Stranded yarn in the Paternayan Persian
 yarn or Appletons crewel wool colors
 listed in the key on page 55
For the bag:
Metal bag frame, 5½" (14cm) across top
20" x 40" (50 x 100cm) coordinating silk
 or taffeta, for lining
Sewing thread to match fabric
Button thread (optional), for stitching the
 bag to the frame

To work the needlepoint

The design is worked in cross-stitch carried over one thread of canvas.

Start at the top right-hand corner and build the pattern outward from there. Work the cross-stitch in rows either across or up and down, but do not mix the two directions. Make sure that all the top stitches run in the same direction. Use 1 strand of Paternayan Persian yarn (or 2 strands of Appletons crewel wool). Work 2 side pieces and 1 gusset piece, following the charts on page 55.

To finish the bag

1 Block the completed canvas pieces, and trim the unstitched canvas margins to ⅝" (1.5cm) all around.

2 Using these pieces as templates, cut out the same 3 shapes in lining fabric.

3 Fold in each end margin of the canvas gusset and press the canvas only.

4 With right sides together, pin and baste the canvas gusset around the curved edge of one canvas side of the bag, starting at the center of the base and moving outward in each direction. Machine stitch or backstitch along the seam. You will need to sew into some of the stitched canvas in order to smooth out the curve in the embroidery around the curved base edges. Check that all the unstitched canvas is covered. Clip into the canvas margin up to the seam every ¾" (2cm) to ease the canvas around the curved edge.

5 Repeat step 4 to sew the opposite side of the canvas gusset to the second canvas side of the bag.

6 Fold in the canvas margins at the top and along the sides. Press and baste.

7 Assemble the lining in the same way. Fold and press the seam allowances for ease of stitching. With the right side out, place the lining inside the bag. Hand stitch the lining to the bag around the top and sides and across the gusset.

8 To make the ruffle, cut out 2 strips of lining fabric, each 1½" x 20" (4 x 50cm). For each strip, fold under ½" (1.5cm) at each end and press. Fold the raw edges lengthwise to the center and press (fig 1). Fold the strip in half lengthwise to hide the raw edges and press. Stitch a gathering thread along the center of the strip (fig 2). Pull up to match the length around the open sides and top of one half of the bag.

9 Hand stitch the ruffle along the gathering seam to the edge of the lining (fig 3) so that it protrudes at the edges.

10 Hand stitch the frame to the bag using buttonhole thread or doubled sewing thread, starting at the center top and working outward (fig 4).

fig 1

fig 2

fig 3

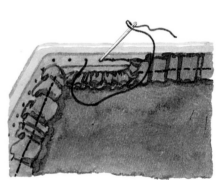

fig 4

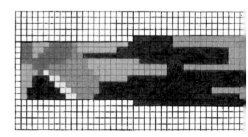

Stranded yarn	Paternayan	Appletons	skeins		black	220	993	3
blue	553	564	2		maroon	900	505	1
gray	202	964	2		deep pink	943	501A	1
honey	734	472	2		pale pink	933	942	1

bag side

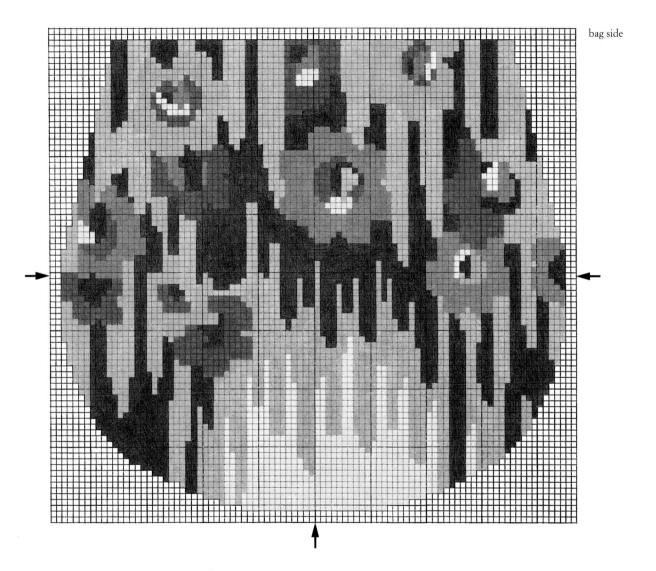

gusset

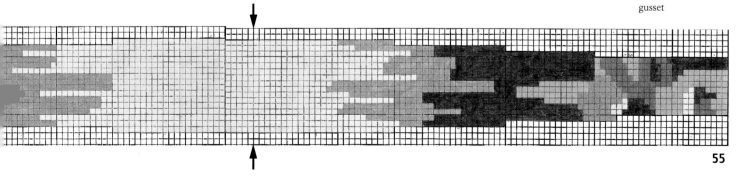

poppy slippers

The idea of your own needlepoint shoes or slippers can be very appealing. Although it is expensive if you have them professionally made up, they should last many years and such unique shoes can be a great pleasure to the wearer.

With their big poppy heads on the toes, these slippers are decidedly feminine, but more masculine motifs can be used to transform slippers into an excellent gift for a man. The Victorians often stitched slippers with animal heads – particularly foxes – on the toes, or with monograms. Plaid patterns are also suitable, and are easy to draw on graph paper before committing the design to canvas. Some pattern sizing is given to enable you to make a pair of slippers to fit; use the outlines as a template to create your own design. The slippers may seem large, but when finished they will be smaller than you might expect.

About the slippers

Approximate finished size: The slippers shown are women's size 4½ and were worked in Rowan tapestry wool.

You will need

For the needlepoint:
10-gauge interlock or mono de luxe canvas, approximately 15" x 20" (38 x 50cm)
Size 18 or 20 tapestry needle
Tapestry wool in the Rowan or Anchor colors listed in the key on page 59
For the slippers:
1 pair round-toed inner soles
Felt
Lining fabric
Binding, for top edge

To work the needlepoint

The design is worked in cross-stitch carried over one thread of canvas.

Work the flowers and foliage first, and then stitch the background. Work the cross-stitch in rows either across or up and down, but do not mix the two directions. Make sure that all the top stitches run in the same direction.

To make the slippers

1 Block the completed canvas and trim the unstitched canvas margin to approximately ¾" (2cm) all around. Use this as a template to cut 2 pieces of lining fabric the same size.
2 Machine stitch the canvas and lining together along the top edge of the needlepoint stitches, leaving ⅝" (1.5cm) unstitched on each side of the center back seam. Trim down the excess canvas and lining to within ¼" (6mm) of the stitched canvas.

3 Pin and machine stitch the center back seam on the needlepoint uppers with right sides together. Trim and press open. Stitch lining uppers center back seam in the same way. Complete stitching around the top edge by hand.
4 Measure around the bottom edge of the finished needlepoint upper, and check that it is ⅛" (3mm) shorter than the outer edge of the inner sole. Using the inner sole as a template, cut 4 pieces of felt the same size.
5 Pin 2 felt soles together, with an inner sole in between. Fold under the canvas around the lower edge of the upper and baste. Trim unstitched canvas to ¼" (6mm). Fit the sole to the base edge of the upper, and keeping the lining edge free, carefully blanket stitch canvas edge to felt sole all around the outer edge, spacing stitches ¼" (6mm) apart.
6 Fold the binding in half over the canvas and lining raw edges. Turn under the raw end of the binding and overlap the other end to join. Hand stitch the binding to the slipper all around. Turn under the lower edge of the lining and slipstitch to the felt inner sole.

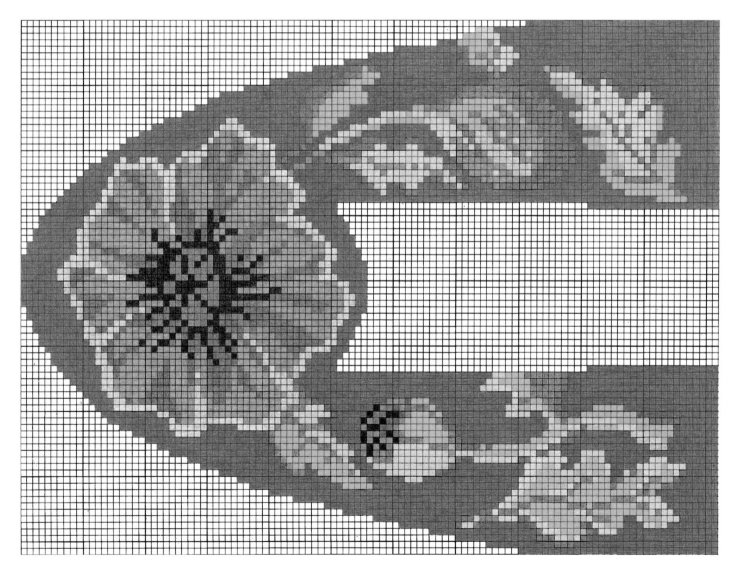

left slipper

Tapestry wool	Rowan	Anchor	skeins
pale orange	C20	8302	2
orange	C22	8232	3
terracotta	J412	8348	1
purple	K423	8528	1
aquamarine	P89	8918	3
emerald	P90	8938	2
bright green	T38	9102	2
charcoal	A625	9798	1
gray-blue	M88	8738	1
royal blue	N57	8692	9

Enlarging the slippers.
Measure around the outer edge of the inner sole
and lengthen the top edge of the upper to this
length minus ⅛″ (3mm). Generally the top edge of
the upper will lengthen by approximately ¼″
(7mm) per size.

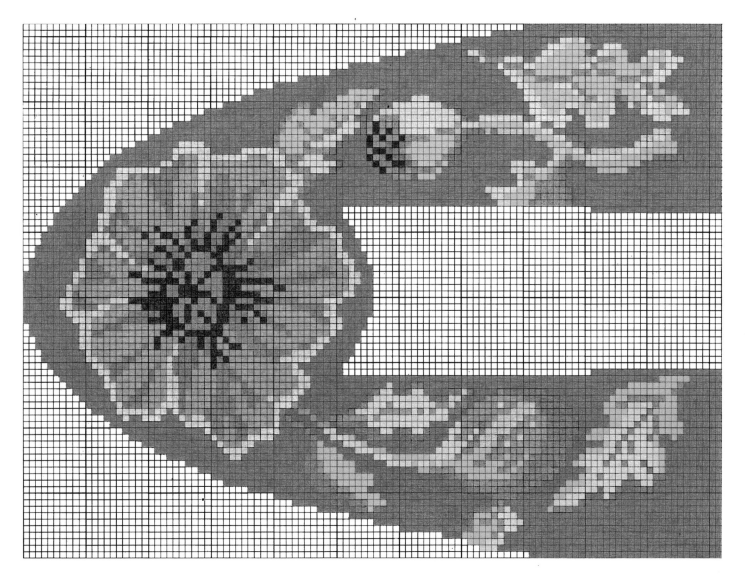

right slipper

Shading

Even in its simplest form, shading can give depth and life to what might otherwise be a flat, dull image. In wool needlepoint, the mat yarn causes the colors to absorb rather than reflect light. Unless some shading is included, the design can be disappointing if it calls for any perspective.

There are a number of ways in which shading can be incorporated into a design without empoying too many colors. For example, when observed closely, the shading on printed textiles and wallpapers may seem crude and the colors surprising, but the results are effective and often painterly. It is the density of the shades – the "tone" – and its juxtaposition to other colors that are more important than the colors themselves. The same approach works well in needlepoint. However, one of the advantages of needlepoint is that no rules apply and the stitcher is free to use as many colors as desired.

shading techniques

Although needlepoint shading can be approached in numerous ways, the three simplest techniques are solid-block shading, which is used for most printed canvases; dotted shading, where the lines are blurred by dotting one color into the next; and mixed-thread shading, where more than one color is threaded into the tapestry needle. All these shading techniques are described below. The most obvious route to shading is to use closely graded colors that move almost imperceptibly from one shade to the next. Hand-painted needlepoint canvases, which can be painted with graded shades, are widely available. Embroidery thread manufacturers' shade cards are often organized into groups to favor this approach.

Solid-block shading

The choice of tones, or color densities, is important when using this method of shading, in which solid blocks of colors are worked next to each other to give the effect of light and dark areas. This method demands some artistic skill and color judgement; for example, the point at which a tablecloth falls from the table edge demands a dramatic change of depth in the cloth color to create the effect of perspective. However, casting a shadow on a petal in order to give it shape and curve usually requires a more subtle change of tone, but not always from the same color group. Looking at paintings shows us that white is often shaded not with gray but with purple, green, or other unexpected hues. The same technique can be applied successfully to needlepoint.

1 Use an ordinary (not colored) pencil to sketch the shapes roughly, and shade them in until you achieve the desired effect. The depth of tone will be shown by the depth of the shading, which will assist you in choosing colors.

2 Stitch the motifs bit by bit, starting with a piece in the main color and then shading it as you go along, in order to build up the picture gradually. Do not stitch all of one color first and then all of the next, and so on.

Dotting

This method of shading consists of mixing one shade into the next by stitching dots of a few stitches of a darker shade into a lighter shade (or vice versa), resulting in a gradual change of color rather than a distinct line between shades. Dotting is especially effective where you need to move quickly from very dark to very light tones. This can be done with any type of thread, and can be used to good effect to enhance printed canvas designs.

1 Stitch the area of the first color, and then work some random stitches of the same color in the canvas still to be worked.
2 Take the second color – which can be dramatically different – and stitch around these dots, then work dots of this color in the next area of unstitched canvas.
3 Fill in around the stitch dots with a third color, and so on.

Mixed-thread shading

This method involves mixing colors to create a graded color change. On small gauge canvases, this can only be done with fine threads or stranded threads that can be separated and mixed and threaded together on the needle. On large 7/8-gauge canvas, two strands of single thread tapestry wool can be used. Depending on the number of threads required to cover the canvas, the new shade can be added strand by strand until a solid color is achieved. Choose shades that are close to one another, and use short lengths only. For example, using three-stranded wool thread:

1 Begin stitching with all three strands of the first color.

2 When you wish to start shading, change one strand to the next shade and continue stitching.

3 Next, change another strand to the next shade to make two strands of the new color, and continue stitching.

4 Finally, change the third strand to the next shade, and continue stitching in the new shade.

You will have moved from one color to the next in several stages. To move through a larger color range, omit step 4 and introduce a third shade, and continue stitching in the same way.

needlepoint bow

Decorative bows are often used in home furnishings to add interest on picture hangers or as a decorative accent to a ring tieback – perhaps to hold a sprig of sweet-smelling lavender. This bow is worked in tent stitch following the colors on a length of ribbon. To echo the feel of a ribbon bow, dotted shading is used to add depth to the twists in the ribbon knot and folds in the bow loops, giving it a three-dimensional effect.

About the bow

Approximate finished size: 9" (22cm). The bow shown was worked in Paternayan Persian yarn.

You will need

For the needlepoint:
10-gauge interlock or mono de luxe canvas, 12" x 15" (30 x 38cm)
Size 18 or 20 tapestry needle
Stranded yarn in the Paternayan Persian yarn or DMC Medici wool colors listed in the key below

For lining the bow:
10" x 12" (25 x 30cm) silk fabric
Sewing thread to match fabric
½" (1.5cm) diameter curtain ring

To work the needlepoint

The design is worked in tent stitch, and the diagonal method is recommended.

Start stitching at the center and work outward. Work the brown dotted shading before filling in the khaki behind it. Use 2 strands of Paternayan Persian yarn (or 2 strands of DMC Medici wool).

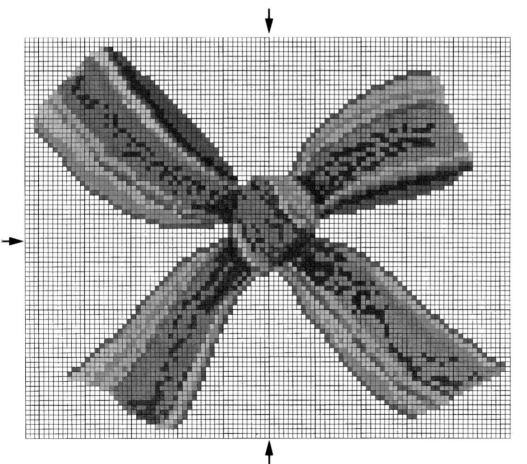

Stranded yarn	Paternayan	DMC Medici	skeins
khaki	453	8501	2
brown	452	8610	1
dark brown	450	8500	1
light turquoise	583	8996	1
bright turquoise	582	8995	1
dark turquoise	580	8993	1
sugar pink	963	8151	1
hot pink	962	8153	1
deep pink	961	8155	1

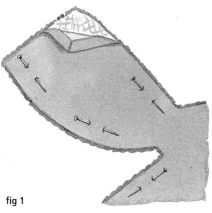

fig 1

To line the bow

1 Trim the canvas around the completed bow, leaving a ½″ (1cm) unstitched canvas margin all around.

2 Cut out the silk lining fabric to the same shape and size as the bow.

3 Turn under the raw edges of the canvas, snipping into the margin as necessary to make it lie flat; baste.

4 Place the needlepoint bow face down on a flat surface and pin the lining fabric to it. Turn under the raw edges of the silk lining to fit the needlepoint bow (fig 1), snipping into the seam allowances as before. Slipstitch the lining to the bow all around.

5 Hand sew the curtain ring to the wrong side of the bow.

patchwork stool top

Using blocks of light or bright colors alongside dark or muted tones can bend the eye's perception and create perspective where none really exists. You need to look closely to see how the colors have been placed to manipulate the light. This deceptively simple but clever shading technique is often used in patchwork, and the design here is taken from the famous "Log Cabin" patchwork pattern. If you plan to substitute colors to fit a different scheme, it is essential that shades of equal tone (depth of color) are chosen to maintain the effect.

About the stool top

Approximate design size: 12½" x 16⅜" (31.5 x 41cm). The stool top shown was worked in DMC tapestry wool.

You will need

For the needlepoint:
10-gauge double-thread (Penelope) canvas, 17" x 21" (43 x 54cm)
Size 18 or 20 tapestry needle
Tapestry wool in the DMC or Anchor colors listed in the key on page 68
For the stool:
Stool with pad 12½" x 16⅜" (31.5 x 41cm)
24" (60cm) of cotton upholstery fabric, 45" (115cm) wide
Sewing thread to match fabric
2yd (1.7m) piping filler cord

To work the needlepoint

The design is worked in tent stitch, and the continental tent-stitch method is recommended.

Stitch the pattern square by square, starting at the top right-hand corner. It is important to work all the stitches in the same direction. This means that on the downward strips of color, stitches are put in side by side. Do not turn the work around to stitch in downward lines, as this will create unevenness and the work may pucker.

Tapestry wool	DMC	Anchor	skeins
dark red	7138	8442	4
salmon pink	7136	8438	2
medium pink	7153	8488	3
light pink	7605	8452	3
pale pink	7132	8394	2
dark violet	7242	8594	1
medium violet	7243	8590	4
lilac	7896	8524	4
blue-gray	7295	8738	2
navy blue	7823	8694	2
turquoise blue	7995	8808	3
light blue	7813	8806	2
pale blue	7301	8814	2
bright yellow	7742	8120	2
pale yellow	7727	8016	2
green	7956	8966	2

To finish the stool cover

1 Block the completed canvas, and trim the unstitched canvas margin to approximately ¾" (2cm) all around.

2 Measure around the needlepoint, and make a length of covered piping cord to this length plus 3" (7cm). Lay the piping on the right side of the needlepoint following step 6 of the instructions for the Circus Pillow on page 28. Pin, baste, and machine stitch around the needlepoint. Then hand sew the ends neatly together to fit.

3 Place the needlepoint on top of the stool, and measure from the top down to the chosen depth. Measure all around the needlepoint top. Cut out 1 piece of fabric to the top circumference measurement plus a ¾" (2cm) seam allowance, by the chosen depth plus 1½" (3.5cm) for seam and hem.

4 Pin, baste, and machine stitch the fabric piece together to form a ring, taking a ⅜" (1cm) seam allowance. Finish the seam allowance, and press the seam open. Turn under a double ⅜" (1cm) hem all around; pin and stitch.

5 With right sides together and the seam positioned centrally in one long side, pin and baste the side piece to the needlepoint. The piping will be caught in between. Using a zipper foot, machine stitch around the edge, keeping close to the piping. Turn the cover right side out. Slide the needlepoint cover over the stool top.

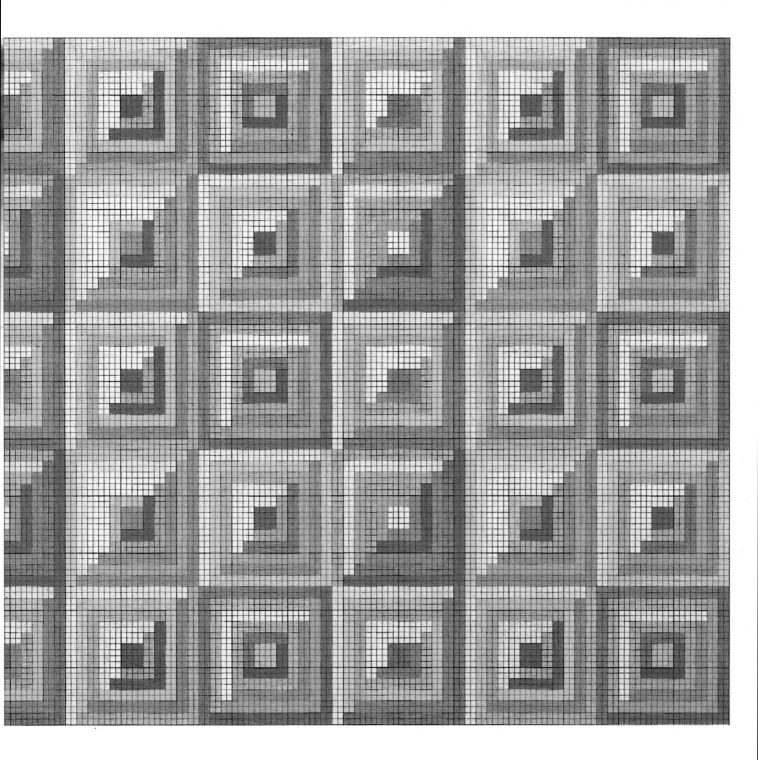

cherub pillow

A classical theme of perching cherubs holding fruits and ribbons makes an appealing design for a pillow that would enhance an old-fashioned drawing room. The colors are soft and subtle, and the shading of the cherubs is worth studying. Note how daring the off-white highlights are – they are not closely graded to the adjacent colors, but are bold and strong. However, the beiges and browns depicting the darker areas are dotted into one another, making the move from one color to the next almost imperceptible. Note, too, how the eyes and mouths are simply suggested with one or two stitches.

fig 1

About the pillow

Approximate finished size: 18" x 9" (45 x 22cm). The pillow shown was worked in Appletons tapestry wool.

You will need

For the needlepoint:
12-gauge interlock or mono de luxe canvas, 24" x 14¾" (60 x 36cm)
Size 20 tapestry needle
Tapestry wool in the Appletons or Anchor colors listed in the key on page 72 and 73
For the pillow:
20" (50cm) square medium-weight cotton upholstery fabric
15" (38cm) matching zipper
Sewing thread to match fabric
1¾yd (1.6m) ruffle trim
18" x 9" (45 x 22cm) pillow form

To work the needlepoint

The design is worked in tent stitch, and the diagonal method is recommended.

Start with the cherubs, leaves, and other features, and then stitch the background all around these worked sections of the design.

To finish the pillow

1 Block the completed canvas, and trim the unstitched canvas margin to approximately ¾" (2cm) all around.
2 Pin and baste the ruffle trim to the front of the pillow cover, gathering the corners a little to insure that they will fan out around the curve (fig 1).
3 Cut out 2 pieces of backing fabric, 20" x 8" (50 x 20cm) and 20" x 4" (50 x 10cm). Insert the zipper in between these 2 pieces, following steps 3 and 4 of the instructions for the Circus Pillow on page 26.
4 With right sides together, pin, baste, and machine stitch the pillow back to the front, sandwiching the ruffle trim in between. For each seam, the needle should run along the last line of stitching, so that no canvas shows and the seam does not encroach on the needlepoint. Trim the seam allowances. Machine stitch around the corners once again, and trim the corners diagonally.
5 Turn the cover right side out, and ease out the corners, using a knitting needle to push them out gently if necessary. Insert the pillow, and close the zipper.

Tapestry wool	Appletons	Anchor	skeins								
dark green	356	7198	2	dusky green	292	9066	2	pale yellow	692	8054	3
mid green	355	9176	1	dark olive	344	9216	1	light brown	762	9326	1
light green	342	9054	1	olive green	333	9306	1	pale brown	761	9324	1
				very pale green	691	9046	1	gray-brown	751	9402	1

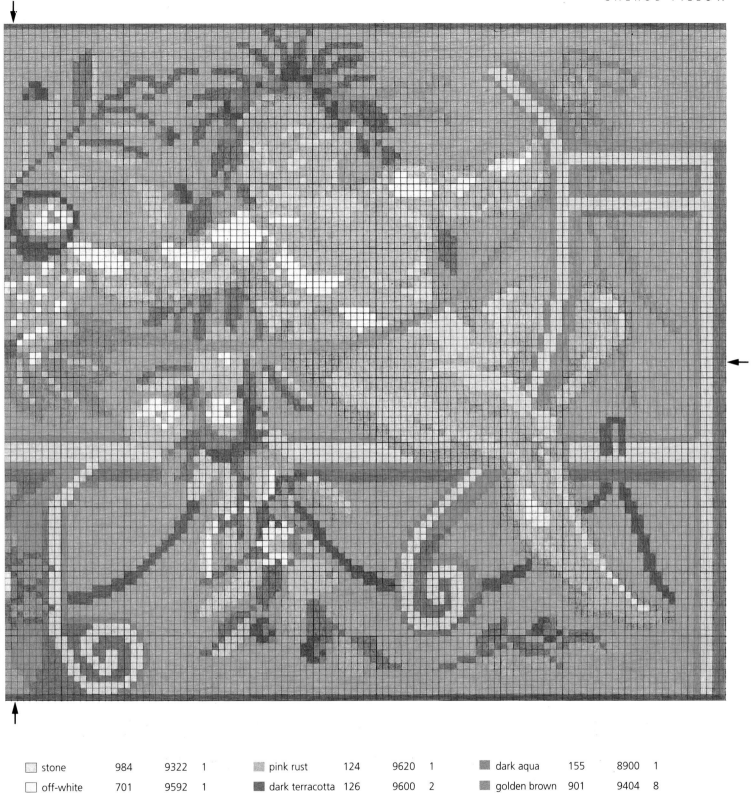

	stone	984	9322	1		pink rust	124	9620	1		dark aqua	155	8900	1
	off-white	701	9592	1		dark terracotta	126	9600	2		golden brown	901	9404	8
	flesh pink	202	9594	2		ginger	696	8102	2					
	dirty pink	121	9596	1		greenish brown	313	9288	2					

Stitch patterns

Although most needlepoint is executed in tent stitch, this is by no means the end of the story. Possibilities for stitch combinations and pattern varieties are endless – textured stitches can be worked on top of smoother stitches, patterns can be made to overlap and interlock, and the use of different canvas gauges, thread types, and color combinations can add further dimensions to the visual effects.

An inventive stitcher may create his or her own stitch patterns to fit a particular purpose. These fancy stitches are rarely suitable for figurative work, but can be used to excellent effect as borders and backgrounds, or as patterns in their own right. Stitching some experimental pieces is well worth the effort in order to keep a record of stitch patterns and the effects they can achieve. Such records are the origins of the traditional "sampler."

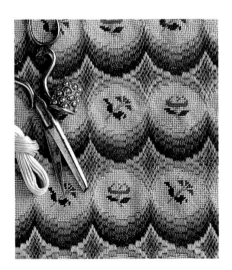

long stitch

Long, straight stitches are easy and quick to make, and long-stitch methods fall into two distinct working techniques. The first is random and may be used to replace the more usual tent stitch where large areas of canvas need to be covered, in wall hangings for example. The second technique is where the stitches are counted to form repeating geometric color patterns worked over regular numbers of threads. This is commonly used where needlepoint is used in the manner of an upholstery fabric, as opposed to pictorial representation.

In the seventeenth century, bed curtains were often worked in long stitch, sometimes with sets of chair-seat covers to match. Long stitches of both methods have the advantage of not pulling the canvas out of shape, but using a frame is strongly recommended to insure an even tension that will result in a flat canvas.

Random long stitch

Random long stitch for small pictures is straightforward to work. The shapes can be filled in with stitches of the required length, and even awkward shapes can be accommodated. If the work is to be framed, single stitches may be as long as necessary, although the longer they are the less they cover the canvas. Doubling the yarn or working very long stitches twice over may be sufficient to overcome this problem. A little experimentation is worthwhile.

For more ambitious pieces, long stitch can be artistically challenging where light and shade, perspective and texture are called for. It is the nearest that

needlepoint gets to painting, and long stitch is currently enjoying popularity. Colors may be mixed in the needle to add highlights or mixed-thread shading (see page 63), or to alleviate the flatness of large areas of single-color stitching.

Stitches should not be made that are too long as they may work loose or snag with use. The length and placement of stitches can also be used to add pattern and textural interest – a technique that requires practice, as there are no set rules to follow. Neither printed canvases nor charts can show every nuance of shade and stitch length that goes into long-stitch designs.

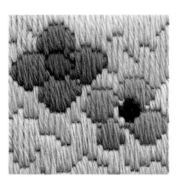

Long stitch used in a straightforward manner to fill in areas of color.

Long stitch using mixed colors and varying stitch lengths to create shading and texture.

bargello

Geometric, counted long-stitch patterns are commonly called Bargello work, although strictly speaking the term applies only to the flame-stitch pattern that is associated with the Palazzo Bargello Museum in Florence, Italy, where four seventeenth-century chairs are worked in a repeating wave-like formation. Traditionally, the bands of patterning are worked in graduated shading from dark to light using one color at a time. This is demonstrated in the Bargello Bolster on page 78, where the repeating pattern consists of five bands of color, each containing five graded shades. Silk threads are often used for highlights in Bargello work, but in old pieces the silk has often disappeared; it is now known that silk and wool "argue," which causes the silk to disintegrate. This is a slow process and should not deter you from using both threads in one piece of work, although cotton embroidery floss is probably safer.

Counted long-stitch patterns

Moving away from traditional Bargello style, endless combinations of geometric counted-thread patterns are possible, from interlocking rectangles and diamonds to cleverly shaded stitch formations that trick the eye to suggest tumbling blocks or woven fabrics.

Straight long stitches are quick to make, and designs consisting of simply shaped, solid blocks of color can be stitched using long stitch in place of the usual tent stitch. The stitches may be even and counted, or randomly stitched to fill an irregular shape. Working in this way takes some practice. Spectacular effects with shading can be achieved by threading two colors together onto the needle. Short stitches are suitable for a wide variety of uses, but long stitches are only suitable for use on items like pictures or wall hangings where the threads will not wear or snag.

Straightforward Bargello-style counted thread stitching in a traditional wave pattern

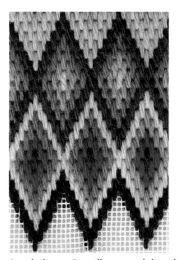
A variation on Bargello counted thread stitching creating interlocking diamonds.

Bargello bolster

This bolster employs one of the simplest of Bargello patterns, with all the stitches carried over the same number of threads. This particular project was stitched by an elderly lady, who bought bags of threads in London's Harrods department store sale every year, and had a natural aptitude for combining colors and shades. The colors are numerous and daring, and not every repeat in the original is exactly the same. When a color has run out, she has used the closest she could find in her workbasket, but she has instinctively used the graded color technique that is typical of Bargello.

fig 1

fig 2

About the bolster

Approximate finished design size: 16" x 20" (40 x 50cm). The bolster shown was worked with scrap wool threads, so the brand is not known. A successful choice of colors is, however, simple to make: select 5 graded shades of each color and put a line of black between each band.

You will need

For the needlepoint:
13-gauge interlock or mono de luxe canvas, 22" x 26" (55 x 65cm)
Size 20 or 22 tapestry needle
Tapestry wool in the Anchor or DMC colors listed in the key on page 81
For the bolster:
Two 21½" x 4" (53 x 10cm) pieces toning fabric
Sewing thread to match fabrics
18" (45cm) bolster, 7" (18cm) in diameter
2 large buttons
1¼ yd (1.2m) piping filler cord
For handmade buttons (optional):
1¼ yd (1.2m) piping filler cord

To work the needlepoint

The design is worked in long stitch carried over 2 threads of canvas. Take care not to stitch too tightly; a frame is recommended.

Starting at the top, stitch the pattern row by row, beginning with a black row. Count the first row carefully and the rest should fall into place.

Always bring the needle up through the canvas below the work (in an empty hole), and push it down to join the bottom of the row above. This will create an even finish and smooth stitches. Also

it is important that the stitches cover the canvas well or holes will show when the finished needlepoint is wrapped around the bolster, spoiling the finish.

To finish the bolster

1 Block the completed canvas well to make it as square as possible, although long stitch usually stays quite straight, making it a good choice for this project.
2 Cut the end fabric in half lengthwise to create 2 strips.
3 Make piping following step 5 of the instructions for the Circus Pillow on page 26. Stitch the piping along the 2 longer edges of the stitched canvas, following step 3 of the instructions for the Strawberry Album Cover on page 30. Place the 2 strips of fabric over the piping, and pin, baste, and machine stitch in position.
4 Next run 2 lines of gathering thread along the raw edge of the fabric at each end (fig 1).
5 Fold the needlepoint in half, with wrong sides facing. Baste the edges of the canvas together, taking care that the edges of the stitching meet as exactly as possible. Also, baste the fabric edges together, to form a long tube with fabric ends. Then machine stitch along the basted seam.
6 Turn the tube right side out, and ease the bolster inside the tube.
7 Pull up the gathering threads on the end pieces as tightly as possible and hand stitch across the gathering with big stitches to hold it in place (fig 2).
8 Sew on buttons to cover the gathered raw edges.

fig 3

To make buttons (optional)

This is not recommended for the inexperienced sewer.

1 Make 2 strips of covered piping cord approximately 16" (40cm) long. Pull up the cord a little to curve the piping naturally.

2 Snip the fabric every ⅜" (1cm) or so up to the seam (fig 3).

3 Wind each length of piping in a circular fashion to make a spiral or "Catherine-wheel" shape, with the raw edges splaying outward. Hand stitch the piping together as you go.

4 When each wheel is a suitable size, tuck the end underneath and snip off the piping. Trim off excess fabric from underneath.

5 Flatten each wheel using a hot steam iron. Tuck the raw edges underneath and flatten again. Turn over and flatten the finished button again.

6 Hand stitch the buttons to the center of the ends of the bolster.

Tapestry wool	Anchor	DMC	skeins
black	9800	7309	3
olive	9068	7377	1
forest green	9028	7387	1
fir-tree green	9078	7396	1
apple green	9094	7382	1
pale green	9058	7400	1
damask rose	8354	7139	1
rust	9602	7212	1
rose pink	8400	7205	1
salmon pink	8306	7760	1
pale salmon	8364	7761	1
dark brown	9622	7468	1
dark gold	8024	7474	1
old gold	8020	7484	1
greeny yellow	9284	7679	1
pale yellow	9192	7501	1
royal purple	8530	7259	1
deep purple	8528	7257	1
mid purple	8526	7255	1
lilac	8524	7253	1
mauve	8522	7896	1
navy blue	8742	7319	1
gray-blue	8738	7593	1
dusky blue	8788	7313	1
light blue	8814	7301	1
pale blue	8714	7284	1

chair seat

This charming pattern is made of oval repeating shapes and combines tent stitch with a Bargello-style surround. It is eminently suitable for chair coverings, pillows, valances, and many other furnishings. However, for dining chairs that are used every day, you may wish to change the long stitches to tent stitch for extra durability.

In this particular piece, which is around 100 years old, the tent-stitch areas have been worked in silk, with the long stitches in crewel wool; the canvas is a soft linen that is rarely found nowadays. Whoever stitched the piece worked with an even tension, because the stitching has caused little distortion to the very soft canvas base.

About the chair seat

Measure your chair to find the design size. The canvas used here is an antique 20-gauge linen canvas. However, since this is extremely fine, difficult to obtain, and too small a gauge for most needlepoint threads, 18-gauge interlock canvas is a good substitute. You may also choose to stitch this design on a much larger scale.

You will need

For the needlepoint:
Canvas of your choice, at least 2½"
    (6cm) larger than finished piece all
    around
Tapestry needle in size to suit gauge of
    canvas chosen
Stranded yarn and cotton floss in the
    colors listed in the key on page 84
For the template:
Square of calico or medium-weight
    cotton, 2" (5cm) larger than finished
    template all around
Waterproof marker pen

To work the needlepoint

1 Make a template of the seat area (see right and page 84), and mark this shape centrally on the canvas.
2 Start by working the top line of long-stitch patterning that frames the top of the tent-stitch roundels.
3 Next work the 4 lines of long-stitch patterning below the roundels.
4 Stitch the flower motifs and their backgrounds in tent stitch – the diagonal or half cross-stitch methods are recommended.
5 Repeat step 2.
6 Work the gold long-stitch patterning that fills the gap created by the ovals.

To make the template

1 Fold the template fabric in half, and mark lightly along the crease. Fold it in half again the other way, and mark lightly along the crease, then fold and mark it diagonally in both directions. This will assist you in placing the fabric centrally.
2 Find the center of the chair seat by measuring diagonally across it in both directions, and then place the fabric centrally on it. Stab a few pins into the seat to hold the fabric. If the seat has a drop front, back, and sides, mark the fabric where it folds under, as these will need to be cut out on the template.
3 Draw a line on the fabric where the upholstery joins the wood, and remove the fabric from chair.
4 Cut the fabric along the marked lines to form the template.

To attach the chair-seat cover

The pattern can be repeated endlessly, and will need to be placed centrally on a template of the item into which it will be made. An upholsterer can make you a template, or you can make your own (see page 82). If the seat needs reupholstering, have it done before making the template, as this may alter the size and shape considerably.

Alternatively, where the upholstery joins the wood, the stitched canvas can be cut to shape, glued and machine stitched to prevent raveling, tacked down, and covered with gimp trim. You can stitch a piece of canvas that is larger all around than the chair seat and let the upholsterer trim it to size.

Stranded yarn	Appletons	DMC Medici
deep pink	227	8114
terracotta	126	8168
light terracotta	206	8166
flesh pink	122	8164
dark green	647	8415
leaf green	294	8414
light green	292	8413
pale green	352	8405
dark gold	696	8303
gold	694	8304
light gold	692	8313

Cotton floss	Anchor	DMC
putty	830	822
dark green	246	319
light green	261	368
dark blue	851	931
light blue	1038	828
terracotta	1015	347
pale pink	1012	948

stitch variations

Stitches other than tent or cross-stitch are useful for speed if large areas need to be covered, and they can also assist in insuring that the piece keeps its shape. Some will fit around tent-stitch features, although slight adjustments may need to be made to the stitch lengths. Many are less flexible and are used in more precisely defined areas.

Most of these stitches and stitch combinations are straightforward if approached step by step, and they can give a piece a textural dimension that not only adds interest but also creates a professional finish.

Rhodes stitch

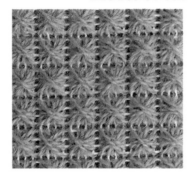

This is a raised filling stitch which covers squares of canvas. It is worked over four threads (using five holes) in each direction. Bring the needle up at A and down at B, up at C and down at D, and so on (fig 1). The final stitch is a full diagonal from one corner to the other (fig 2).

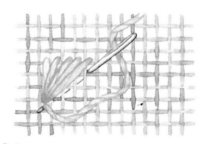

fig 1

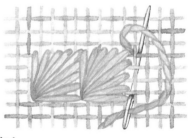

fig 2

Fan stitch

This stitch consists of nine straight stitches fanning out from a single hole to create a square, worked over four threads (figs 3 and 4).

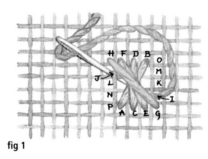

fig 3

fig 4

Star stitch

Star stitch is constructed with eight straight stitches radiating out from a central point (fig 5). The stitches can be made over two canvas threads (fig 6) or three.

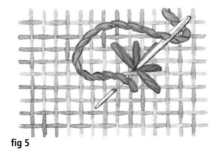

fig 5

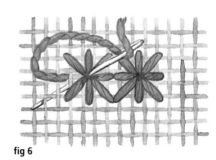

fig 6

Gobelin filling stitch

This is a useful alternative to tent stitch for large backgrounds. The number of threads it is worked over can be adjusted to suit the application. The stitches are worked in interlocking rows (fig 7). Bring the needle up through the canvas below the previous row (in an empty hole), and take it down between the stitches of the previous row (fig 8). There are many different versions of Gobelin stitch, each one based on straight stitches arranged in various directions to cover large areas of canvas. A combination of colors can be used to add another dimension to a stitched piece.

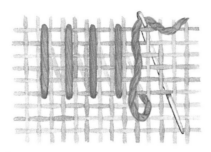

fig 7

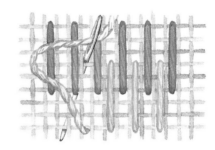

fig 8

Milanese stitch

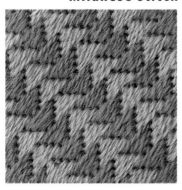

Used over a large area, this stitch creates an interesting texture – an effect that may be lost if the stitch is not allowed enough space. The triangular pattern consists of four stitches of graded length, set in diagonal rows pointing in opposite directions (fig 9). The stitches are constructed in the same way as satin stitch, and the triangles are stitched one at a time, working diagonally across the canvas and back (fig 10).

fig 9

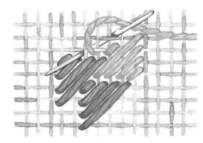

fig 10

Hungarian stitch

This stitch consists of rows of vertical stitches worked in repeating sets of stitches made over two, four, and two canvas threads (fig 11). Each row is worked to fit into the preceding one. Stitching alternate rows in a second color will add an interesting textured effect (fig 12).

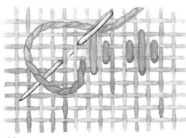

fig 11

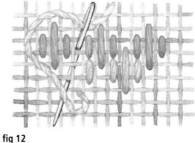

fig 12

87

evening purse

This simple-to-make but very effective purse uses a stitch pattern that prevents the finished canvas from being pulled out of shape. The pattern for this piece is made of squares of stitches intentionally facing in different directions in a planned formation. The first square is worked with the stitches starting from the top left-hand corner, the adjacent squares are stitched starting from the top right-hand corner, and so on, creating a subtle checkerboard effect as the light falls on the different directions of the stitched squares. This texture is further emphasized by the sheen of the cotton floss used for the project. The beads are added at the end as a decorative touch.

About the purse

Approximate finished size: 8" x 5½" (20 x 14cm). The purse shown was worked in Anchor cotton floss.

You will need

For the needlepoint:
14-gauge interlock or mono de luxe
   canvas, 12" x 18" (30 x 45cm)
Size 20 or 22 tapestry needle
Cotton floss in the Anchor or DMC
   colors listed in the key on page 91
Fine sewing needle, to fit through your
   chosen beads
Strong gold sewing thread
320 small gold-tinted glass beads
For the purse:
15" x 8" (38 x 20cm) batting
17" x 9½" (43 x 24cm) lining fabric
Sewing thread to match fabric
Large snap and strong sewing thread
   (optional)

To work the needlepoint

This pattern is best worked using diagonal tent stitch and is a good piece on which to start if you are unfamiliar with this method of stitching.

Work the squares first, starting at the top and working one square at a time, until the piece consists of 8 x 16 squares and measures about 8" x 16" (20 x 40cm). Each square is 12 x 12 stitches.

Add the border, starting with 2 rows of oblong cross-stitch, followed by an interlocking long-stitch pattern. When working the long stitch, try to insure that the threads lie flat, not twisted, across the canvas.

Finish with 2 rows of tent stitch, worked in alternate directions to keep the canvas straight. Fill the corners with Rhodes stitch as shown on page 86.

Use 6 strands of cotton floss throughout.

To work the embroidery and beading

The flowers are embroidered on top of the points where 4 squares meet on the front section of the purse (fig 1). Stitch the red buds first, using long stitch. The 2 leaves are lazy daisy stitches, and the stalks are 3 small stem stitches (fig 2). Flowers are not stitched on the back section of the purse, but beads are placed where the squares of stitching intersect (fig 3).

The beads are sewn on using backstitch, which helps prevent them from hanging loose. Bring the needle and thread up through the canvas, thread on the bead, then complete the stitch. Keep all the stitches facing in the same direction, so that the beads lie evenly. On the border, beads are sewn on between every other cross-stitch; on the flowers, on leaf tips and buds.

To finish the purse

1 With right sides together and the canvas uppermost, machine stitch the lining to the stitched canvas, leaving an opening of 6" (15cm) along one of the shorter sides. The needle should run along the center of the holes containing the last line of stitching for the front

flap. For the rest of the bag, stitch along the first row of empty canvas. Experiment along one side first to check that the stitches are correctly aligned.

2 Trim the canvas and lining to ⅜" (1cm) all around, and trim the corners diagonally to insure a crisp finish.

3 Turn the purse right side out, and gently ease out the corners using a knitting needle.

4 Push the batting in through the opening, and flatten it out inside the purse. Slipstitch the opening closed.

5 Fold up approximately 5" (12cm) of the front section. Using gold cotton floss and a tapestry needle, oversew the edges together, stitching into the holes of the canvas.

6 If you would like a fastener, use strong sewing thread and a sharp needle to sew a snap to the inside front and a matching point on the front of the purse, stitching carefully between the stitches.

Note: To adjust the size of the finished piece, increase the number of stitches in each square. Alternatively, you can add more squares, but the width must be made of an even number of squares in order to accommodate the surface embroidery of flowers and beads.

fig 1

fig 2

fig 3

Cotton floss	Anchor	DMC	skeins
gold	363	976	23*
dark red	1005	815	1
dark green	224	500	1

* 1 skein is sufficient to stitch 7 squares of 12 x 12 stitches

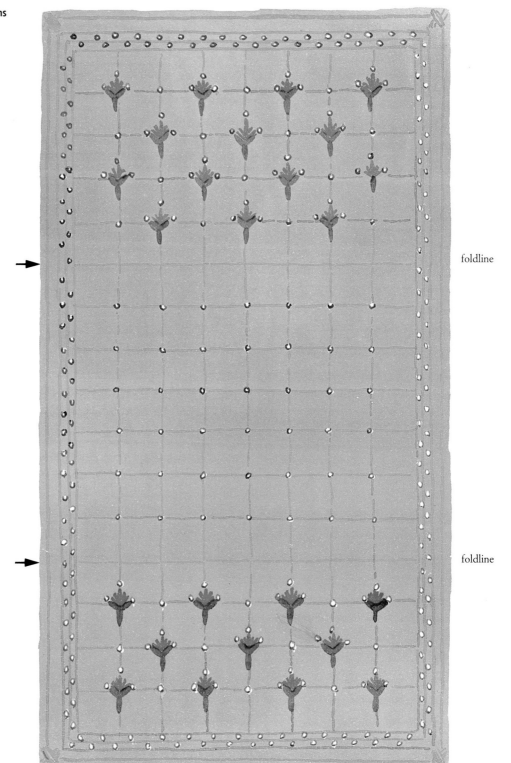

foldline

foldline

91

sampler

This stitch sampler employs 36 stitch combinations, each contained inside a square with 25 holes (24 threads) in each direction. The challenge is to make these stitch patterns fit together with some semblance of order. Note, too, how the stitch patterns and color combinations of this sampler have been chosen to balance the whole design. Stitching a sampler produces familiarity with the disciplines and restrictions.that stitch combinations impose, and this can inspire invention.

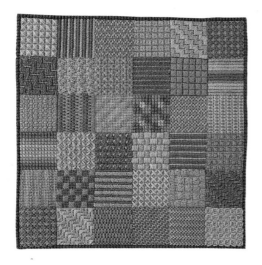

About the sampler
Approximate design size: 10¾" (27.5cm) square. The sampler shown was worked in Paternayan Persian yarn.

You will need
14-gauge interlock or mono de luxe canvas, 20" (50cm) square
Size 20 tapestry needle
Stranded yarn in the Paternayan Persian yarn or Appletons crewel wool colors listed in the key on page 96

To work the needlepoint
It is important to count out the patterns on a piece of graph paper before committing them to canvas – it is very frustrating to find that the stitches will not fit evenly into the designated space. For this reason, it is also a good idea to work a stitch-patterned or geometric border before stitching the center, to insure that it fits. Sometimes a little "cheating" is necessary in order to achieve a fit.

This design is also suitable for a pillow, but two or three rows of tent stitch in the darkest shade should be added around the edge so that it can be made into a finished item without spoiling the stitching.

Use the layout plan on page 96 as a guide to which stitch to use in each square. Mark the center of the canvas and work the squares one at a time, starting with the 4 central squares and working outward.

The layout plan on page 96 is also a guide to the number of canvas threads each stitch is worked over.

To finish the sampler
Block the completed canvas before framing. Do not trim the unstitched canvas border, because the framer will need a good margin of canvas to wrap around the backing board.

To make the sampler into a pillow, follow the instructions for finishing the Circus Pillow on pages 26 and 28.

Stranded wool		Paternayan	Appletons	skeins
	pale blue	213	875	3
	grey	506	561	3
	bright blue	554	462	3
	steel blue	504	743	3
	dark blue	502	746	1

Working the patterns

Eight of the thirty-six stitch combinations are illustrated with diagrams to help get you started. The remaining twenty-eight are only summarily described.

3 Straight stitch and tent stitch combination

Work the straight stitches first, and then fill in the tent sttiches. Note how the tent stitches face in different directions to create chevron shapes.

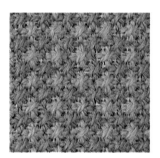

6 Upright cross-stitch, doubled

Start with a cross-stitch made over 4 canvas threads and worked horizontally and vertically. Work a second stitch over the top, over 2 canvas threads, in the more usual diagonal formation.

8 Christmas tree stitch on tent stitch

Work the tent-stitch background first, taking care to angle the stitches as illustrated. This is important for creating the symmetry required for stitching the Christmas trees on the top.

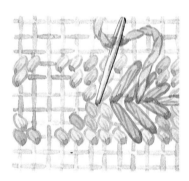

9 Rice stitch

This stitch is made up of large cross stitches worked over 4 canvas threads with diagonal stitches worked over the arms of the cross-stitches, over 2 canvas threads.

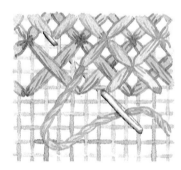

10 Fly stitch

Fly stitch is like chain stitch but with an open rather than a closed end. Here the stitches are worked close together and with a short anchoring stitch. In square 35 they are spaced out, leaving an empty hole between the stitches and with long anchoring stitches that adjoin.

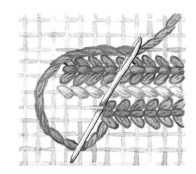

15 Tent stitch with French knots

This pattern consists of 4-stitch squares of tent stitch with French knots at the corners. To make a French knot, bring the needle up at the knot position. With the needle pointing away from you, twist the threads around it once. Put the needle down again where it emerged and pull through firmly, holding the thread taut with your left hand.

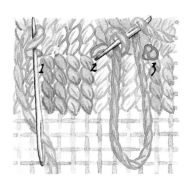

20 Star stitch variation

This complicated looking, and very decorative, pattern is simpler than it looks. Work the base star stitches first and then the big crosses over the top. Finish by anchoring down the centers of the cross-stitches with straight stitches over 2 canvas threads.

23 Plait stitch and tent stitch combination

Work a row of tent stitch, then plait, then tent stitch, and so on. The plait stitch rows are worked from left to right.

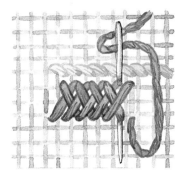

Stitch combinations Use this as a true sampler and experiment with your own combinations and choice of threads. It is easier to stick to four or five colors to prevent the design from becoming unbalanced, but there are no rules. For a good result map out the design on graph paper before starting.

1 Rhodes stitch, see page 86
2 Straight stitch worked over 2 threads
3 Straight stitch and tent stitch, see page 94
4 Star stitch, overlaid with second color
5 Byzantine stitch worked over 3 threads
6 Upright cross stitch, doubled, see page 94
7 Jacquard stitch worked over 1 and 3 threads
8 Christmas tree stitch and tent stitch, see page 94
9 Rice Stitch, see page 94
10 Fly stitch worked over 2 threads, divided by tent stitch, see page 95
11 Satin stitch squares worked over 4 threads with each block separated by backstitch

12 Diagonal straight stitch worked over 2 threads
13 Satin stitch squares worked over 3 threads, divided by backstitches worked over 3 threads
14 Gobelin stitch worked over 4 threads
15 Tent stitch worked over 4 threads, in alternate directions with French knots, see page 95
16 Cross-stitch worked over 2 threads with top stitches worked in alternate directions, see page 50
17 Straight stitch worked over 2 and 4 threads
18 Double oblong cross-stitch worked over 2 threads with an extra straight stitch in between, see page 51
19 Cross-stitch worked over 2 threads, see page 50
20 Star stitch variation, see page 95
21 Large cross-stitch worked over 4 threads with double French knots
22 Straight stitch worked over 4 threads overlaid with backstitching worked over 3 threads
23 Plait stitch divided by tent stitch, see page 95
24 Reversed double cross-stitch worked over 3 threads and divided by tent stitch
25 Tent stitch worked in alternate directions and overlaid with backstitch, see page 22
26 Checker stitch worked over 4 threads
27 Diagonal long stitch
28 Cross-stitch combination worked over 4 threads
29 Fan stitch, see page 86
30 Half Milanese stitch
31 Hungarian stitch, see page 87
32 Milanese stitch, see page 87
33 Gobelin stitch
34 Diagonal tent stitch, see page 22
35 Fly stitch
36 Star stitch worked over 2 threads, see page 86

Charts & motifs

The following pages offer a range of additional charts and design
motifs which will complement the projects in the earlier chapters,
and provide inspiration for you to develop further needlepoint
patterns of your own. They include charts and keys for two boat
pictures: a steamer and a yacht and additional patterns for a hand
and a heart pillow. Fruit, vegetables, and flower motifs, a collection
of counted border patterns, and a selection of different backgrounds
will help you increase your needlepoint repertoire.

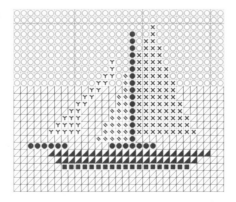

seaside pictures

See Boat Pictures on page 24

Complete a trio of boat pictures by working these two designs, following the charts and keys for colors and threads. The motifs on the near right can be used, same size or enlarged, as single images or reduced to form a border for one of the boat pictures.

Steamer

Cotton floss		Anchor	DMC	skeins
●	black	403	310	1
■	red	9046	817	1
Y	brown	374	3828	1
↘	orange	316	971	1
○	sky gray	922	3768	1
╱	sea gray	851	924	1

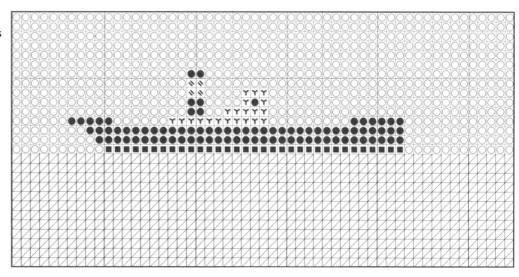

Yacht

Tapestry wool		Rowan	Anchor	skeins
■	maroon	H659	8512	1
◢	dirty pink	J412	8348	1
●	brown	X146	9392	1
×	off-white	B84	9362	1
↘	cream	A2	8006	1
Y	white	A110	8002	1
╱	sea blue	M415	8792	1
○	sky blue	M422	8834	1

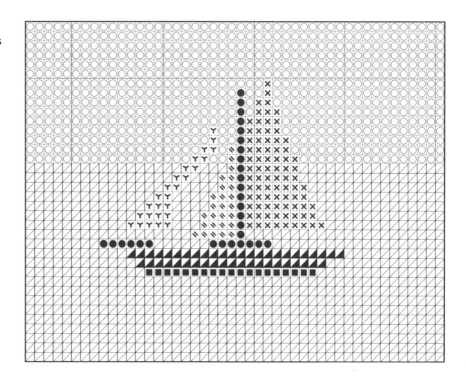

99

hand & heart

See House, Heart & Hand Pillows on page 44

These additional patterns are for the hand and heart designs in this set of three pillows. Trace the shapes and areas of stitch pattern, and enlarge to your chosen size. Mark the outlines onto the canvas following the instructions on page 15. Use the same thread colors as for the House Pillow, combining shades together to achieve a subtle faded effect.

fruit &
vegetables

This collection of fun motifs, similar in style to the teacosy on page 36, can be enlarged or reduced on a photocopier to the size of your choice. The motifs can then be used as a single design or arranged in groups to create free-form borders or allover patterns.

flower motifs

Flowers are ideal motifs for needlepoint. This selection of different blooms can be used in the size shown here, reduced for working on fine canvases for smaller projects such as pincushions, or enlarged to fit seat covers or pictures. Look at the colorings of the Bobble-edged Pillow, page 40, or the Poppy Slippers, page 56, for inspiration when choosing thread colors for your flower pieces.

backgrounds

Large areas of background can be made more interesting both to stitch and to look at by adding some very simple patterning. It is a general rule that the thread colors should not vary too greatly. However, with single "dots" a high contrast, such as white dots on a dark background,can work really well. Choose the main needlepoint motif, then design a background that contrasts in color and effect.

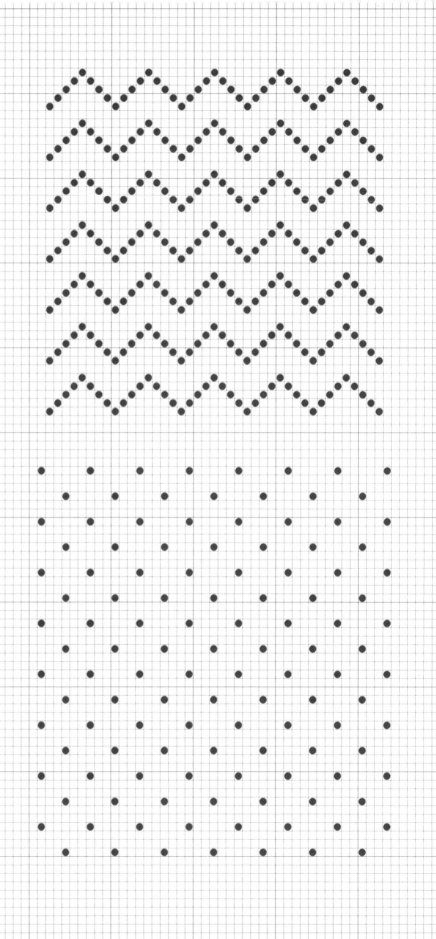

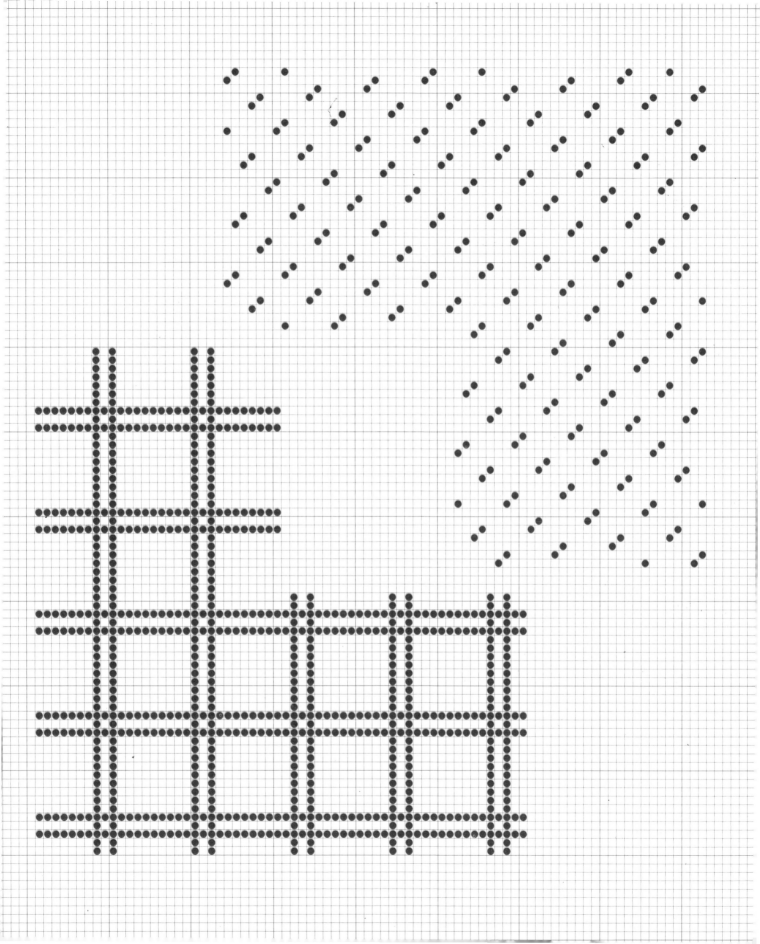

border patterns

This selection of repeating "counted" border patterns can be translated in a variety of different ways. The patterns, near right, are based on single-stitch arrangements, while the patterns on the far right, are long-stitch designs. These patterns can also be used as allover designs for cushion covers and chair seats, in a similar way to the Kelim Pillow on page 32.

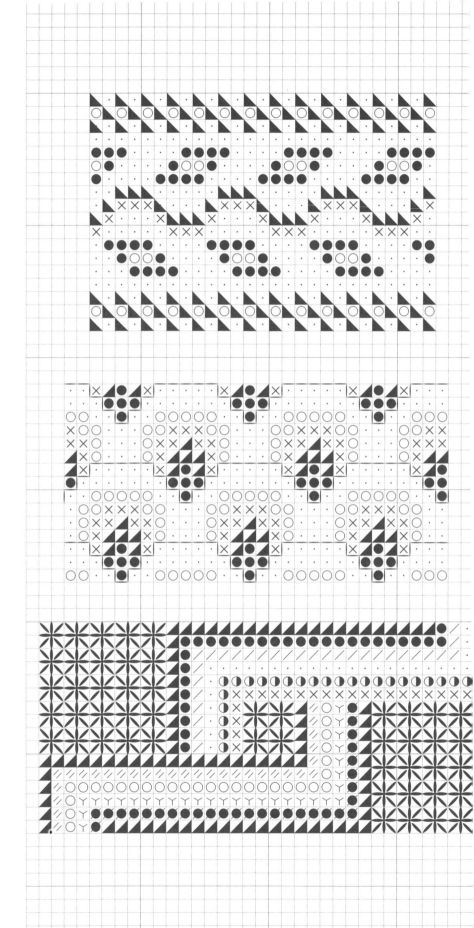

index

acknowledgments

The author would like to acknowledge Kathryn Whitefoot's invaluable assistance with the stitching of the sampler and the slippers. Thanks are also due to Sarah Ross Goobey for lending the antique needlepoint used for the chair seat, to Paterna Persian Yarn for stitching the art deco purse so beautifully, to Cara Ackerman at DMC, and Julie Gill at Coats who were both extremely helpful in providing materials and technical advice.

The publisher would like to thank the designers and stitchers who contributed the following projects: Candace Bahouth for the Kelim Pillow (page 32), DMC for stitching the Patchwork Stool (page 66) from a design by Susan Duckworth, Jan Eaton for the Needlepoint bow (page 64), Lucinda Ganderton for the Album Cover (page 30) and the Heart, House and Hand Pillows (page 44), Jolly Red for the Circus Pillow (page 26), and the Tea Cozy (page 36), Gill Speirs (La Toison d'Or) for the Bobble-edged Pillow (page 40) and the Cherub Pillow (page 70), Victor Stuart Graham for the Boat pictures (page 24).
The Evening Purse (page 88) and the Sampler (page 92) were designed and stitched by the author.

The publisher would also like to thank Sally Harding for her invaluable editorial assistance, Christine Hanscomb for the use of her cottage as a location, Veronique Rolland for assisting the photographer and Antonia Gaunt (and her dog, Kivu) for the styling.